The Problem
of the Perrigo Patriots
# of Pownal

The Problem of the Perrigo Patriots of Pownal

A Genealogy of the Perrigo Family

in Colonial New England

Virgil E. Raines

Compass Flower Press
Columbia, Missouri

Cover Map LOC image credit:

Jefferys, Thomas, -1771. A map of the most inhabited part of New England, containing the provinces of Massachusets Bay and New Hampshire, with the colonies of Conecticut and Rhode Island, divided into counties and townships: The whole composed from actual surveys and its situation adjusted by astronomical observations. [London Thos. Jefferys, 1774] Map. https://www.loc.gov/item/74692162/.

Published by
Compass Flower Press
Columbia, Missouri

Library of Congress Control Number: 2024915193
ISBN: 978-1-951960-64-3

Table of Contents

Preface

I undertook this project knowing that other researchers have already contributed in many ways to our understanding of the lineage of the Missouri Perrigo line, and I am indebted to them for those efforts. I will recognize them appropriately throughout the book. Despite those many contributions to published and unpublished records, there remain many unknowns, and blank lines in genealogy charts, not to mention a couple of published mistakes. Furthermore, information concerning the historical, geographic, political, and religious settings is essential in gaining a complete understanding of why things happened as they did. I have endeavored to bring those dimensions into view. This project is much more than a genealogical chart with boxes and dates. I intend to tell not only the "what and when" of my ancestors' lives, but I will offer up some of the "why did it happen" dimension.

The geographic setting for much of this book is centered around colonial Massachusetts, Connecticut, and New Jersey. Many of the European settlers came to those shores seeking religious freedom. We will see how those various religious institutions, or the lack of them, impacted the early Perrigo family. It has been suggested to me to leave the religious issues on the cutting-room floor and focus on information that people care about. Those recommendations were a polite way of telling me that I run the risk of angering a few people if I discuss religion. The title of the chapter "Witches and Baptists Need Not Apply" might be an example of such a controversial topic. I chose to leave that chapter intact as I believe that history shows that a Presbyterian or Baptist might not readily fit into the setting of territorial religious fiefdoms of early rural Massachusetts. If you lived in Boston in 1730, religious affiliations were not as emotional an issue as one would find in the counties to the south or north. Remember, the founding fathers of Massachusetts mostly lived in Boston, and some were not that religious in their beliefs and activities. It was much different in Plymouth County to the south, and even in Connecticut. This story bears that statement out. I do not wish to offend anyone, but I believe that witches and Baptists sometimes had a hard time fitting into the early rural Massachusetts setting. And no, I do not believe the Perrigos were witches.

I think you will see that this Perrigo family went the extra mile to prove their worth and fit into the newly founded democracy.

About the Author

Colonel (U.S. Army Retired) Virgil E. (Sonny) Raines was born in Jackson County, Missouri, (North Kansas City) to V. Elwood Raines and Ruby Nadine Adams/Raines. He was raised on a farm in Shelby County, Missouri, attended school there, and graduated from Paris High School in Paris, Missouri. He enlisted in the army during the Vietnam war and obtained a commission as a second lieutenant. He became an army aviator, served in several overseas assignments, and commanded from captain to colonel level during his nearly thirty-year career. His overseas assignments included Vietnam, Thailand, Korea, Germany, Saudi Arabia, and Turkey. He graduated from Park University and the University of Pennsylvania with multiple degrees and is a graduate of the Army Command and General Staff College and the Army War College. He has served on several college faculties and as a professor of military science at the U.S. Naval War College. He has published articles on the war on drugs, several technical articles on military aviation, and several books: *Footprints of the Painter and Scott Families of Missouri* and *Horse Sense—William Rains and the Missouri Seventh Volunteer Cavalry*. His soon-to-be-published book *Beat Your Drum Loudly* is a book of family patriots. He has also published several short articles on family members who served in the Second World War. Virgil is a member of the Sons of the American Revolution and teaches genealogy research to potential DAR and SAR members as well as to patients at veterans' homes.

His wife, Emma Jo Painter/Raines, was born in Monroe County, Missouri, to Oliver and Lita Blanche Scott/Painter, attended school there, and graduated from Paris High School. She graduated from GEM City College and worked in the defense industry until her husband's military service began. She has worked as a Department of the Army and Department of the Navy civilian and as an accountant. She has served in her chapter of the Daughters of the American Revolution as chapter regent and as registrar for several years.

The Raineses live on a farm in Boone County, Missouri, and have three children and seven grandchildren.

Chapter One

Why This Book?

Our Raines/Adams family connection to the Perrigo line is well documented for at least four generations prior to my generation by other family members. My maternal grandmother was Blanche Francis Perrigo Adams. I remember this kind lady as she spoiled my brothers and sisters and myself. Great memories. I also vaguely remember her father, Andrew Jackson Perrigo (1873–1957). My first exposure to him was possibly in 1948, and he seemed to be a very kind man, but sad. Later, I came to understand one of his sons had recently been killed in World War II and that he had just lost his wife, Stella, that year. His family was a "Gold Star" and a "Red Star" family of that war. Two of their sons served in heavy combat, one losing his life. Son Woodrow was killed in the European theater near the end of the war in 1945. I have published an account of his service. His brother Wilbur served in the Pacific theater in the navy, and I have also published an account of his service.

Andrew's father was Martin Vanburen Perrigo (1840–1923), who was born in Adams County, Illinois, and moved to Shelby County, Missouri, where he farmed and spent the remainder of his life. His father was Justus Perrigo Jr. (1816–1886), also of Adams County, Illinois. Justus Jr. served in the Civil War in the Missouri Black Hawk regiment and then later in an Illinois regiment. Those family connections are well documented by other family members. The father of Justus Jr. was of course Justus Perrigo Sr., also of Adams County, Illinois.

Justus Perrigo Sr. was born in 1768 in Pownal, Vermont. He was a bit young for the Revolutionary War but certainly would have been aware that several close family members served in that conflict. He did, however, serve in the War of 1812 in New York and was involved in heavy fighting while in the army. He was injured several times and discharged because of those injuries; accordingly, he was declared disabled by the army when discharged. He received a land grant for that service in what was to become Adams County, Illinois. Some of what was to become Adams County was designated as land grant territory, and present-day Quincy is in Adams County. It appears from newspaper stories that Justus was not one of the first settlers in Adams County, but the first, possibly in 1822 or earlier. We have some interesting stories about Justus. He was recognized in a newspaper article as an "Old Soldier" and was killed in a riverboat accident in 1833 on the Mississippi River.

We have a copy of a letter he sent a prospective bride in Illinois describing his large orchard and the richness of his land. She soon joined him in that "Garden of Eden." Adding to the mystery, Justus moved to Adams County with adult sons later to follow him, including Justus Jr., so we can assume he had a previous marriage. We have not found records of that marriage, nor do we know his previous wife's name. His children gave New York as their birth location in post-1850 federal census reports.

Our family has been uncertain of the father of Justus Sr. My research over the years focused on David Perrigo being his father, but it was an unproven relationship. My work pointed to David Perrigo, a well-known Revolutionary War Patriot, but later research established that this David was too young to be the father of Justus. Over the years, this mystery has attracted the attention of several family researchers, all more accomplished than I, with limited results. Who was he?

My approach to this mystery has been to start our research with the first American generations of the Perrigo family and take a hard look at the entire lot of them. In military terms, shoot them all down and sort them out on the ground one at a time. This broad approach has yielded some interesting stories about a tough family that has been known to fight a good fight. Several fights.

I want to recognize the work of a family member, the late Professor Robert "Bob" Bishop of Florida. Robert published two volumes of Perrigo family history from 1979–1982 BC (before computers) in which he documented the family line as best as he could, given the time allotted. There were many other family researchers who contributed to this body of knowledge, including my mother. This research project is listed in the reference section of this book and will be referred to as the "Perrigo Papers." I have those documents, but the question remains after all that research: Who was the father of Justus Sr.?

As an aid to future researchers, we have included the references used in our study of this family at the end of this book. As the American Perrigo line grew and spread from Connecticut, New Jersey, Massachusetts, Vermont, and New York, I focused on the line that likely produced Justus because of the Pownal connection. Figure 3 below is a modified family pedigree chart starting with the first American generation and ending with the fifth generation. There are a lot of names, boxes, and dates, but this will prove useful in following the family tree as I develop the family groups and stories with each generation. Notice that I have made note of the general location of each family member for the first four generations. This will help in getting to know the persons bearing the often-used given names of Robert, James, Ezekiel, John, and David.

It is in the third American Perrigo generation that we find several connections with Pownal, Vermont. It is in Bennington County, the southwestern corner of the then territory, near both the colonies of Massachusetts and New York. It was settled in the mid-1700s by the British and was home to a volatile mix of tough colonists, Tories, and people that just wanted to be left alone. An early description I found of the town mentioned there was not a church or meeting hall, and the people were unfriendly and did not trust outsiders. This was a logging area, and there had been schemes in which land speculators sold land based on New York documents and British land claims. The colony of New York was also laying claims to Vermont territory land. There were ample reasons to not trust outsiders.

We have several records of Perrigo family activities from Pownal: census reports, petitions, military records, and published reference books. Several Perrigo men served in the Revolutionary War in state and local militias in and around Pownal. The multi-generational uses of common given names presented us with the problem of sorting them into the correct family lines and generation and then finding the father of Justus Perrigo Sr. Therefore, we so approach *The Problem of the Perrigo Patriots of Pownal*, an appropriate name for this book.

The historical setting in which most of this book is based is pre-colonial New England. This was a much different place than post-revolution New England. Many of the early Massachusetts settlers during the pre-1700 era were seeking religious freedom. Not freedom from religion, but to exercise their right to choose a religion. There were several religions making an American start in Massachusetts, and they at first tended to be territorial. I am not sure the early Perrigo family came to America for religious freedom as much as for financial freedom. While we will see them associated with several different religions, we will find the Baptist Church most often mentioned as a place of marriage. I am sure that Baptists did not fit smoothly into the Puritan communities of early Massachusetts. The same can be said for Dutch and Scottish communities. I think the Perrigo family tried to fit in, but there were obstacles. You will see those obstacles play out as we progress through the generations.

I had little difficulty locating birth, marriage, and death records in the Boston area in the pre-revolution era, as by 1700, the major towns or cities were very efficient in maintaining those records. You may have been married in a church, but you most assuredly marched down to the city hall and recorded that marriage or intent to marry. The same applied to births and deaths. I suppose in the case of death, someone else performed that function.

One line of the family settled in New Jersey after leaving Connecticut. Records are more difficult to locate in pre-revolution New Jersey. In fact, colony and federal census reports for 1790 and 1800 certainly missed some Perrigos, actually nearly all of them. Marriage records were especially difficult to locate. I found a reference that seemed to explain these difficulties. The book *Documents Relating to the Colonial History of the State of New Jersey*, Volume XXII, Marriage Records 1685–1800, listed in the Reference Section, relates the many challenges of marriage regulation in the early colonies. The various religions brought their own rules pertaining to marriage, and these rules varied greatly from one religion to another. In pre-colonial Massachusetts, marriage quickly became a state affair. Marry in a church if you so choose, but record it at city hall. New Jersey became a haven for several religions that were not so quick to allow marriage to become a state affair, hence there was a loss of documentation as churches merged or died out. There were plenty of rules. For example, a woman marrying for the second time could not wear her wedding dress from the first marriage. Bear in mind a wedding dress was probably the only decent piece of clothing that woman possessed. It would not have been a wedding dress we would envision today. That dress was not her property to wear at such an occasion. The above reference did not contain records of any Perrigo marriages for a period of 115 years, yet we can be certain there were Perrigo marriages in that state.

It appears that, given the fact that the Perrigo family did not belong to one of the several religions with strict marriage policies, they often used the services of a justice of the peace and went on with their lives. Many of those records simply did not survive.

A short discussion of the spelling of the Perrigo surname is needed. It was probably spelled "Perigo" and often "Perigoe" in England, and this spelling persisted after the family's arrival in Connecticut. The second *r* seems to have been quickly added, however, and that spelling was the version most often found during my research. Rest assured, I found a bunch of other ways to spell this name, but those versions did not seem to stick. I believe most of the first fifth-generation family members were quite literate and could sign their own documents, hence the name was not "Americanized," and spelling errors sometimes seen in early American documents were not often found. I elected to use the most common spelling in this book. I should note that within a certain New Jersey line I found several family groups that insisted on the Perigo version, and I have noted that variation where appropriate. That version seemed to stick with that line.

Chapter Two

Baystater, Nutmegger, Garden Stater, or Flatlander?

I was taught that the Perrigo line from which I descended was French. That is partially correct, but the first-generation Perrigo in this line immigrated from England. That was a two-generation stopover as the family moved from France. Robert Bishop, who edited and published the Perrigo Papers listed in the Reference Section below, discussed that there were two Perrigo lines that settled in the colonies: one from England and one from France. This project will focus on the English line from which I am descended, starting with the first American generation in the 1650s in New England. I believe the French line first settled in Baltimore and Virginia.

Throughout this book I will refer to the various New England pre-revolution and post-revolution colonies, and the various counties within each colony. It will be useful to consider the colonial boundaries at the time of the Perrigo family arrival in the 1650s and then after the state lines were eventually drawn with their counties. Figures 1 and 2 add clarity to that effort.

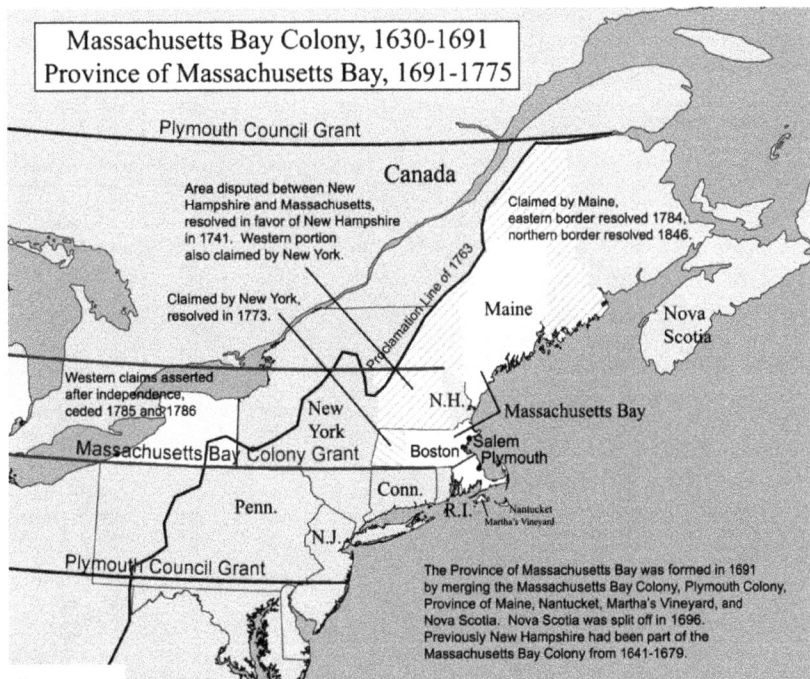

Source: Wikimedia,
Kmusser, 27 Sept 2006.

FIGURE 1: Massachusetts Bay Colony 1630–1691

Map labels:

MAINE
Aroostook
Piscataquis
Somerset
Penobscot
Franklin
Washington
Oxford
Kennebec
Waldo
Hancock
Andro-scoggin
Knox
Lincoln
Cumberland
Sagadahoc
York

VERMONT
Grand Isle
Franklin
Orleans
Essex
Lamoille
Chittenden
Caledonia
Washington
Addison
Orange
Rutland
Windsor
Bennington
Windham

NEW HAMPSHIRE
Coos
Grafton
Carroll
Belknap
Sullivan
Merrimack
Strafford
Cheshire
Hillsborough
Rockingham

Pownal

MASSACHUSETTS
Franklin
Essex
Middlesex
Hampshire
Worcester
Berkshire
Suffolk
Norfolk
Hampden
Plymouth
Bristol
Barnstable
Dukes
Nantucket

CONNECTICUT
Litchfield
Tolland
Windham
Hartford
New Haven
Middlesex
New London
Fairfield

RHODE ISLAND
Providence
Kent
Washington
Bristol
Newport

FIGURE 2: New England Map

In later chapters I will portray the location of each family group and where they were born, got married, fought, and died. In some instances, the information is quite general or misleading, such as that given in military records, but more on that later. Figure 2 above presents the various present-day New England counties. Of course, county lines have changed over time, but the general locations of these counties have not. New England county lines did not change drastically after the Revolution as did, for example, Kentucky county lines, so Figure 2 is good enough for the intended purpose. This statement is supported by two studies I have located that examine those changes. Those resources are listed in the Reference Section below.

The first-generation Perrigo family was in Saybrook Township, Middlesex County, Connecticut. By the second generation, we see them living in the Boston area and in Piscataway Township in Middlesex, New Jersey, and then in Rhode Island and Pownal, Vermont by the Revolutionary War. All these locations, except for Pownal, are near the coast, and less than 150 miles from the Saybrook home.

This story will show the family migration north and west. The family pedigree chart in Figure 3 partially depicts that movement by showing the colonies of residence for each family group. Keep in mind that over the five generations examined in this project, the various family groups did not move far. Although no scales are shown on the maps, the distance from Lyme, Connecticut, to Boston, Massachusetts, was less than 110 miles, and one would pass through Rhode Island on the way to Boston. The distance from Suffolk, Massachusetts, to Pownal, Vermont, is less than 150 miles. Because of these relatively short distances, I am inclined to believe that the various family groups over the several generations were in regular contact. It would also explain why we see family members serving in the military in Connecticut while their families were in neighboring Massachusetts. This probably differs from other post-revolution migration of families finding themselves in Oregon thirty years after leaving Virginia and family groups losing contact forever.

One can imagine that the primary motivation for a family to relocate in this era would be the availability of land. That is the question I have considered while conducting the research for this project. I am sure that was a major factor, but there were other issues to consider. The first-generation Perrigos were seafarers. They owned land, but probably just enough to grow their food. Robert Perrigo Sr. sold some land, and it was described as land with dung upon it by the man purchasing that small plot in Lyme. He probably had a few hogs. Some of the third-generation families may have been quite poor, and land ownership for them was not so likely. Two families were "warned out" of Massachusetts towns for that reason. By the fourth generation, we see the same families being professional retailers and belonging to professional organizations. They were beginning to enjoy "The American Dream." By late in the fourth generation, we see four of these family groups living on the frontier and owning land. Now they had something to fight for, and they did just that.

I discovered an early Mansfield, Connecticut, First Baptist Church record from the 1750s listing several Perrigo family members. The members of this congregation voted to move from

Mansfield to Newton, Sussex County, New Jersey, to practice their religion in a manner of their choosing. Within the Connecticut church, they had differing beliefs about baptism, and they voted with their feet. This was a group move and probably involved the family of second-generation Ezekiel Perrigo (1658–1724). Ezekiel was dead by this time, and he had lived in New Jersey since prior to 1700, but it was likely his Connecticut descendants that made that move. It was about a 180-mile move. I think that religious beliefs were a factor for the Ezekiel Perrigo line's move from Connecticut to New Jersey. The location for this move was not Piscataway but Sussex County, in northwest New Jersey. The livelihood of several of these family groups was not primarily agriculture. I found shoemakers, clockmakers, and loggers in this family. One man lost his life in what was likely a logging operation. That is not to say they had no interest in agriculture, but I suspect that it took a couple of generations for the family groups to acquire enough wealth to purchase farmland. I am certain that Pownal, Vermont, offered that possibility.

Because several of the family groups lived in Pownal, Vermont, I want to provide insight into what that frontier town and region might have been like. *A Gazetteer of Vermont*, shown in the Reference Section below, gave an interesting description of Pownal and Bennington County in the late 1700s. It described the soil as being generally good and producing plentiful crops. The Hoosic River has its beginning near Pownal and flows northwest to Hoosic, New York. Along that stream were fertile farms that provided needed grain. This reference described that in 1762 there were four or five Dutch families within the limits of the township owning land granted by the government of New York based on the "Hoosic Patent." In 1762, the goods produced consisted of wheat, Indian corn, potatoes, hay, maple sugar, and wool. The 1771 Vermont census discussed elsewhere in the book reported eleven families living in Pownal in 1762–77. This was not a large town when James, John, and David Perrigo first settled there, and its economy was based on agriculture beyond that of subsistence living. We will see Perrigos applying for land grants in Vermont.

Figure 3 depicts five generations of Perrigo family groups and where they lived. This will aid in understanding the family histories in the following chapters. I found it difficult to understand which generation the various Davids, Johns, and Jameses discussed in the Perrigo Papers and the "Cutter Account" belonged to. The *Genealogical and Family History of Northern New York,* written by William Richard Cutter, is referred to as the "Cutter Account" throughout this book. This chart will help in that endeavor as we proceed through history. This chart does not depict all the female descendants of Robert Perrigo, but I have included most of them and their important stories along with their respective family groups.

England
Connecticut

Robert
Perrigo
1624-1683
Sarah Smart
Marah Wood

Connecticut
New Jersey

Ezekiel
1658-1724
Alice Elsey
Mary Webb?

Connecticut
Massachusetts

Robert Jr.
1661-1711

Mary

New Jersey

Thomas
1699-1724

New Jersey
Massachusetts

David
1701-1746
Catherine
Alsop

Massachusetts

Ezekiel
1701-1779
Susanna Wilson
Sarah Farnham
Ann Wooster

Massachusetts
Vermont

James
1702-1786
Lydia Hayward*

Connecticut
Massachusetts

John
1698-1783
No Children
Elizabeth
Wilson

New Jersey
New York

Joseph
1745-1840
Annie Platt

Massachusetts

John Kemp
1735-1757
No
Children

Massachusetts

David Jr.
1736-1780
Abigail Brock

John
1745-
1747

Massachusetts
Rhode Island
New York

Robert
1729-1808
Susannah H
Sarah
Shorey

Massachusetts

James Jr.
1731-1808
Eliz.
Dickerman
Eliz. Pettee
Thankful W.

Massachusetts
New York
Vermont

John
1733-1812
Mary Flint?

Massachusetts
Vermont

David
1738-1804
Susanna
Varrel

David 1771
Abel 1773-1865
Joseph 1774-1864
James 1776-1850
Isaac 1782-1864
Samuel 1787-1830
Margaret 1791-1843
Elizabeth 1792-1861
Annie 1794-?
Eleazer 1799-1878

Ezekiel 1758-1803**
David III 1760-?
Molly Tripp 1763-?
John 1764-1820
Abigail 1767-?
Elizabeth 1771-?
Sarah 1774-?

Joseph Hewes
1743-1843
Dr. Robert Jr.
1765-1829

John 1773-?
James III
1774-?
Jared 1775-?
Molly 1777-?
Elizabeth
1777-?
Robert 1779-?

Elijah 1758-?
Polly 1760-?
Rufus 1761-?
David 1757-?
Dr. John
1767-?
Silvester
1768-?
Sally 1788-?

Frederick H 1765-?
Justus J. 1768-?
Charles
1779-?
William 1772-?

Underlined text reflects Revolutionary
War Patriot
*Mayflower Descendant
**Wife was a Mayflower Descendant

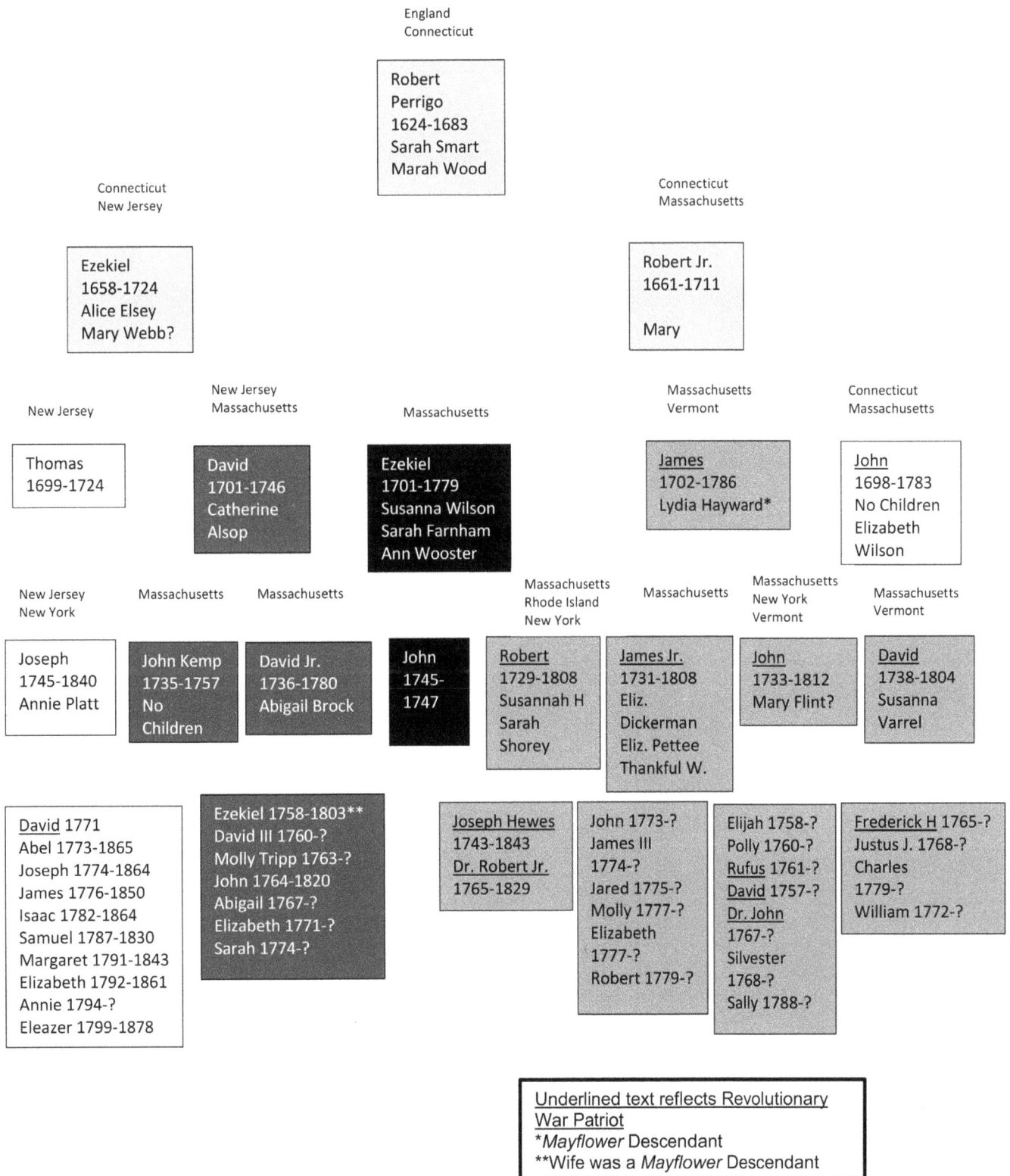

FIGURE 3: Five Generations of the Perrigo Family Tree

Chapter Three

"One Day This Swamp Will Be Yours"
The First Two Generations

Generation One

Robert Perrigo Sr.

Born: 15 December 1624

Died: 18 April 1683, Old Lyme, Connecticut

Birthplace: Hastings, Sussex, England (Baptism date)

Married: (1) Sarah Elizabeth Smart on 8 August 1657 at St Michael's in Barbados and (2) Mary (Marah) Wood circa 1670

Buried: Unknown but probably in Old Lyme, Connecticut

Robert was the son of John Perigoe (1588–1662) and Amie Gregorye Scott (1589–1630) of Hastings, Sussex, England. The East Sussex, England, Church of England Baptismal Index gives the date of birth and the name of his father. John was a fisherman of the port city of Hastings, which might explain son Robert's career choice of seafaring. Figure 4 below is a listing of the fishermen of Hastings, which includes John Perigoe. Source: "Historic Hastings" described in the Reference Section. I found several documents supporting this spelling of their name in England.

John Perigoe's father was Robert Perigoe (circa 1560–1617) also of Hastings, Sussex, England. His wife was Martha Gabryell (1560–1645). Robert Perigoe may have been born in Picardie, France, and was a blacksmith/gunsmith. Figure 5 below shows that John was a gunsmith, and he probably produced some of the weapons on this list of Hastings's weapons resources. Source: "Historic Hastings" described in the Reference Section.

John had a record of criminal history in addition to being a gunsmith. On 1 February 1585 he was found guilty of theft and allowed benefit of clergy. He seems to have been found guilty of burglary in Hastings on at least two later occasions and was hanged after the third conviction at Norden's Cross in Hastings in 1617. I have an article, "The Trials and Tribulations of Robert Perigoe," published in the *Sussex Family Historian* in March 1994. (See the Reference Section). This case was complex and remindful of current-day scandals involving businessmen, but he broke the law a little too often and did pay the price. I make no excuses for Robert, but he was not a career criminal, although he probably behaved in an unacceptable manner even by today's standards, not to mention the standards of that tremulous period of British history. Another incident involved a young woman and an out-of-wedlock birth.

The first American-generation Robert Sr. was an early settler in Saybrook, Middlesex County, which was later set off as Lyme, New London County, Connecticut. He was a mariner who served on "Goodall's" ship. His maritime operations were based in Boston. He would have been in his mid- to late twenties upon his arrival soon after his first marriage to Sarah Smart in Barbados in 1657. We have records of several land transactions in Saybrook, some as early as 1659, so his arrival in the colonies would have likely been prior to that date. One transaction listed in the book *Saybrook at the Mouth of the Connecticut River: The First One Hundred Years* documents that he bought three and three-quarters acres on 16 January 1659. His children were all born in Saybrook, with the earliest born in 1658. They were:

- Ezekiel, 22 June 1658 to 22 July 1724
- Robert Jr., 1661–1711. Line from which Justus Sr. descended.
- Sarah Royce, 29 November 1665 to 1728. Married John Royce, a prominent Connecticut political leader and founder of Windham, Connecticut.
- Anna Creese, born 31 March 1674. Married John Creese (1661–1729).
- Mary Downing, born 1 April 1677, died 1737. Married Jonathan Downing (1677–1729).
- Abigail, born 21 July 1681 and possibly died in 1683.
- Elizabeth, born 30 October 1683. Born six months after the death of her father, Robert. She died by 1691 and was not alive at the time of her father's probate case suit of 1711.

Sarah Elizabeth died in 1672, so the four final children were born of his second wife, Mary. After his death, Mary married Robert Peterson, who outlived her. Robert Perrigo left Mary sixty-three acres of land, and her surviving second husband, Robert Peterson, then retained possession of that land after her death. It is likely that the Perrigo children claimed their rights to that land according to a will we have been unable to find. This action was filed in 1711, years after his death, and settled in 1719 in the children's favor. It is also important to remember that Mary lived until 1719 and that Robert's will may well have allowed her the use of that property until her death. Note that three of the children—Abigail, Elizabeth, and Robert Jr.—were dead by 1711. Robert Peterson claimed to have paid the surviving children for that land but could not prove his claim. The 1719 court summons for the surviving children is an excellent source for the names of these family members.

We have records of Robert Sr.'s christening in England listing his father and mother, as well as records for his marriage to Sarah Smart. We also have an excellent written account of his life by Byron Nelson that describes him as a mariner and explains that his operations were based in Boston and that he was absent from home on several occasions. This story lists some of the court cases in which he was involved and lists his children. This list is not in agreement with the names of the children we found in estate documents; however, the death of two children prior to the estate case explains some of the confusion. The court summons also mentions James, who is probably a grandson, son of Robert Jr.

Robert Sr.'s first wife, Sarah, was seemingly a businessperson. I found the minutes of the Court of Burgomasters and Schepens in New Amsterdam (originally part of Connecticut), in which Sarah was listed in a defendant in a suit brought by Joris Dopzen on 24 May 1663. During the first session the plaintiff appeared drunk in court, and the case was continued until 5 June 1663. During the latter session the plaintiff's wife testified that she had one hundred guilders of tobacco that had been attached by Sarah Perrigo for a debt owed to her by Dirck Jansen, who was to receive the tobacco from the plaintiff. Sarah was ordered to deliver the tobacco to Jansen. Sarah would need to file against Jansen to obtain payment. We can speculate that Robert Perrigo was away on a voyage and that when he returned later that year, he filed suit against Jansen. I have found records of a suit filed by Robert later that year but could not determine the details.

Figure 6 below is a map of New London County, Connecticut, depicting the location of Old Lyme Township, Connecticut. Lyme was split off from Saybrook about the time of Robert's arrival. The official time of the split of Old Lyme from Lyme may have been as late as 1850, but some much earlier documents reflect Old Lyme. This map also shows parts of Middlesex County with Old Saybrook adjacent to Lyme. We have also found records of the Perrigos from Essex Township in Middlesex County.

John Perigoe
Fisherman in Hastings, Sussex, England in 1623

APPENDIX II

HASTINGS FISHERMEN IN 1623

The following list is taken from a return of " The names of the Seamen inhabiting w'thin the town and port of Hasting " dated iij April, 1623, in the Public Record Office (SP. 14/142/24). Many of the names are still to be found in the town today:

William Seale als Gynner	Mark Phillip	Robert Scott
Marke Black	John Sargeant jun	William Stan'
Steven Duke	John Meadow	Robert Arthur
Edward Bartholomew	John Fawteley his serv't	Henry Coombes
Robert Bartholomew	Robert Puntes	John Phillip
John Joye sen	Mark Puntes	Mark Luckett jun
Edward Palmer	Richard Hyde	John Coxe
Thomas Kitchin	Michael Hyde his son	Thomas Luckett
Robert Phillip jun	Peter Winckfeild	Samuel Gawen
John Michell sen	Daniel Winckfeild	— Penvocle his serv't
John Howlett	Michael Wright	James Luckett

Robert Lovell	Richard Sargent	Mark Luckett
John Perigoe	Thomas Rowland	Mark Luckett sen
Xpr Joye jun	Geffrey Gawen	John Guy
John Joye jun	John Gawen his son	James Chowll
Marke Joye	Richard Gawen	William son of Steven Gawen
Peter Stanbynorth	John Bosam	Steven Haddon
Mark Haddon	Mark White	John Salmon
Thomas Stryde	Anthony Waters	John Lowll
John Fawteley sen	Robert Phillip sen	Mark Sargant jun
Henry Palmer	John Bayley jun	John Whelpdale
William Reignold	William Phillip	John Grygge
John Boys	Thomas Wood	Henry Steven
Thomas Wright	Robert Nicholas	Thomas Joye
Richard Barrey	James Wood	John Aynett
Edward Lote	Mark Barrey	Henry Chepman
John Lote	Richard Penvocle	Thomas Winckfeild
Robert Wright	William Alesbury	Michael Earle
George Fellow	Robert Tought	John Luckett
Richard Wheeler	John Fawteley jun	Edward Sargent
John Wheeler his son	James Wright	William Sargent his son
Robert Pymme	Thomas Gawen	Thomas Rowes his serv't
James Crosse	Steven Gawen his son	Thomas Coosens
Paul Standybnorth	John Gawen	Thomas Palmer jun
Simon Boys	Thomas Moore	Moses Earle
Thomas Wales	John Barry	Robert Palmer
Edward Sparow	John Smyth	Thomas Elmes
John Sparrow	John Mabb	Richard White
Richard Coosens	John Hyde	Nicholas Palmer
Nicholas Daniell	John Bayley sen	John Sargent sen
John Chowll	John Bosam	John Sargent
Mark Sargiant sen	Edward Bartholomew sen	Thomas Sargent } his sons
Thomas Sargiant his son	Simon Bourne	Anthony Midimore
Robert Sargiant	John Steven	Daniel Larey
Mark Sargiant his son	Thomas Rowes	Andrew Page
Thomas Palmer	Henry Tyers	Robert White
Thomas Palmer his son	William Chepman	Thomas Page his serv't
Mathew Moore	John Chepman his son	John Tompsett
Peter Bourne	William Chepman	Thomas White
John Woodford	Mark Wright	Michael Cloyden
Edward White sen	John Ball	John Luccas
William Gawen sen	Xpofer Bosam	Andrew Steven
John Austin	Henry Bosam	

oric
Hastings

J. MANWARING BAINES, F.F.S.A.
Parish Clerk of All Saints and St. Clements and onetime Curator of the Hastings Museums

1986
PUBLISHED BY
Cinque Port Press Ltd
ST. LEONARDS-ON-SEA, EAST SUSSEX

John Perigoe - Fisherman: This text; Appendix II, pages 356 and 357 of Baines, 1986, lists 156 Seamen residing in Hastings in April, 1623. John Perigoe lived his entire life in Hastings. He was baptised on July 7th, 1588 in Saint Clements Church in Hastings and died at the age of 74 on October 15th, 1662 in Hastings. He would have been 34 years old at the time of this listing, married and father of four young children. One more child, Robert, would be born the following year in 1624.

Baines cites his source as "Public Record Office, (SP. 14/142/24)."

Compiled 03/

FIGURE 4: Fishermen of Hastings, Sussex, England, 1626

A return of the general musters held at Hastings in September, 1614,[33] gives a detailed

list of names together with the equipment each provided. Here are the first 15 out of the 301 entries, in tabular form:

		Corslet	Musket	Pair of Curets	Caliver
John Akehurst	Mayor	1	1	1	
James Lasher	Jurat		2	1	
Martin Lyf	. .		1	1	
William Byshop	. .	1	1	1	
Rich. Wytheris	. .	2	2	1	
Thomas Young	. .	1	1		
Clement Whitfield	. .	3	3		
Richard Waller	. .		1	1	1
Jeremy Bryham	. .		1	1	1
Richard Boys	. .		1	1	
William Parker	Minister	1	1		
Harbert Pelham	Esq		1	1	
Lawrence Pierse	Esq	2	2	1	
Thomas Delves	Gent	1	1	1	
Edward Bennet	Clark		1		

The total equipment was 26 corslets (body armour), 94 muskets, 32 pairs of curets (the front breastplate was called a cuirass, and both front and back plates a pair of curets), 20 calivers (light muskets fired without rests), 9 halberds, 4 bastard muskets, 153 bills and sculls, 1 axe, 3 caps and 32 dry pikes. James Bachelor and Thomas Mose were the surgeons, Thomas Fuller and Robert Perrigoe " gunnesmyths ", and Sabb. Stevenson the " Droom ".

Historic

Hastings

J. MANWARING BAINES, F.S.A.

*Parish Clerk of All Saints and St. Clement and
onetime Curator of the Hastings Museums*

1986
PUBLISHED BY
Cinque Port Press Ltd
ST. LEONARDS-ON-SEA, EAST SUSSEX

Robert Perrigoe - Gunnesmyth: This text; from pages 191 and 192 of Historic Hastings, Baines, 1986; describes the mustering of citizens of Hastings in 1614. In addition to the list of individuals mustered, it inventories the armament of the group and lists specific individuals who provided support services (2 surgeons, 2 gunsmiths and a "Droom"). Robert Perrigoe is listed as one of the two gunnesmyths (gunsmiths). In another part of this book Robert Perigoe's occupation is listed as "Blacksmith" which would be consistent with this entry. Robert Perigoe was born in Sussex some time before 1550 and was hung for burglary in Hastings in 1617.

Robert's surname is shown as both Perigoe and Perrigoe in this book. Most records spell the name with one "r", Perigoe, at this time.

Baines cites his source as "Public Record Office, SP, dated September 30th, 1614".

Compiled 03/14/2018

FIGURE 5: Historic Hastings Gunsmith, 1614

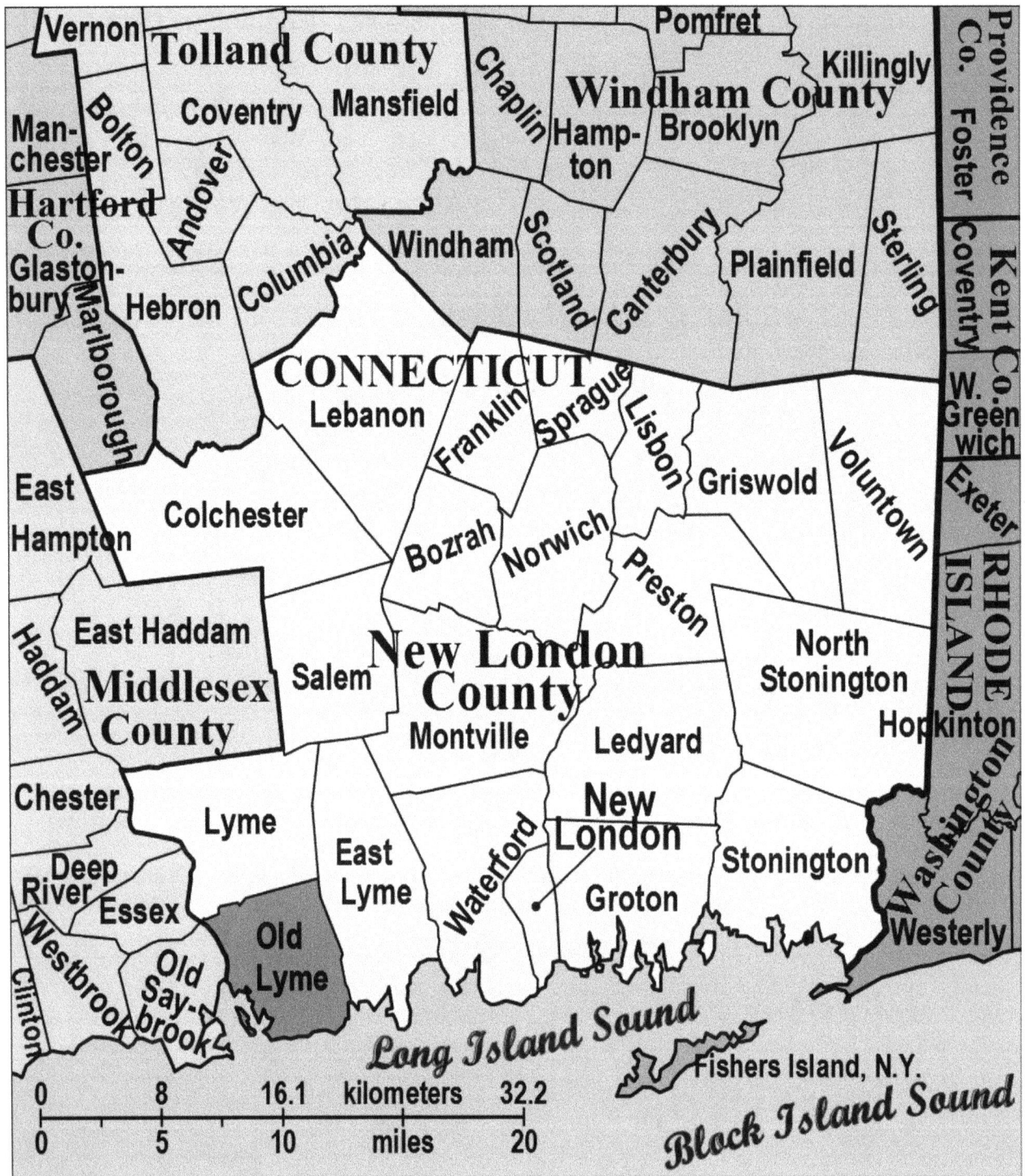

FIGURE 6: Old Lyme, New London County, Connecticut

The history of Saybrook Township in colonial Connecticut at the time of Robert Perrigo Sr.'s arrival in the mid-1650s helps us understand the living conditions of these early settlers and the social, economic, and religious influences on their lives. The book *History of Middlesex County, Connecticut* listed in the Reference Section gives a detailed look at these influences from 1635 to about 1850.

The early settlement of Saybrook started at Ft. Saybrook at the mouth of the Connecticut River with Saybrook on one side of the river and what was to become Old Lyme on the other. This was home for the Perrigos. These early settlers first dealt with the Indian tribes by buying their land and later taking it from them. They then dealt with the New York colony and their claims. In addition to these problems, there were a lot of rules for citizens to follow: how to handle livestock, how to take wild game, and how to manage almost every aspect of their lives were established by local county and township governing councils. Then there were religious practices. By 1700, the population had grown, and settlers began movement to the west and south into New Jersey. I noticed that one large church in Saybrook made the decision to make a congregational move to the west, which greatly depopulated Saybrook to the point that loss of tax revenue threatened the survival of the town. I discuss later in the book such a move of a First Baptist Church from Connecticut to New Jersey. Descendants of Ezekiel Perrigo discussed next were probably members of that congregation. This church is discussed in depth later in the book, as it helped me document the New Jersey Perrigo line.

It was clear that some of these early settlers were desirous of greater freedom or more security than what was offered by the early Saybrook settlement. Thus, we see one Perrigo line move to New Jersey and one to the Boston area, which might have seemed to be more secure. Second-generation Ezekiel moved to New Jersey, and his brother Robert Jr. moved to Massachusetts. Their sisters either remained in Connecticut or moved to New Jersey. Their stories follow.

Generation Two

Ezekiel Perrigo
Born: 22 June 1658
Died: 22 July 1724, Piscataway, Middlesex, New Jersey
Birthplace: Saybrook/Lyme, Connecticut
Married: (1) Allice Elsey on 18 December 1695 and questionably (2) Mary Webb on 3 February 1706
Buried: Unknown location

Ezekiel was the son of Robert Perrigo and Sarah Smart and was born in Lyme, Connecticut. I have records of his birth in Connecticut and estate documents of his death in New Jersey. He was also shown as a resident of New Jersey in 1719 in the court summons for his father's estate. The *Genealogical and Family History of Northern New York* will be referred to as the "Cutter Account" throughout this book. It was written by William Richard Cutter and is shown in the below references. This account states that Ezekiel served as a soldier in 1707 in Northampton. I believe his service to be in support of Queen Anne's War. This was a war involving England, France, and Spain, with some fighting in the colonies and Canada. We are uncertain where he enlisted, but he likely served in New Jersey and Massachusetts, with Northampton being in Massachusetts. His service is also shown in the *Genealogical Guide to the Early Settlers of America* which is shown in the Reference Section.

I have his marriage records recording his marriage to Allice Elsey on 18 December 1695 in Piscataway, New Jersey. However, I question his marriage to Mary Webb in Northampton, Hampshire, Massachusetts, in 1707 despite the fact that I have those records. Furthermore, I have Mary's family records including birth and parents' names in Northampton. The Cutter Account and the Perrigo Papers as well as the *Genealogical Guide to the Early Settlers of America* make this claim, but it makes little sense as I believe his wife Allice Elsey was still alive at the writing of his will in 1724 and that he named her as the executrix of that will. Experienced researchers would simply conclude there were two Ezekiel Perrigos, and that is true. This second Ezekiel was a third-generation Perrigo and a son of Robert Jr., the brother of this Ezekiel. The second Ezekiel married Susanna Wilson, which is proven with his story told later in the book. I will leave the mystery of the spare Ezekiel to future researchers, as my Perrigo search has netted no candidates. The children named in his 1724 will were:

- Sarah Chandler, 1699–1724
- Thomas Perrigo, 1699–1724
- David Perrigo, 1701–1746
- Alice (Alis or Elsie) Perrigo, 1710–1764

I have the Piscataway, New Jersey, birth records for his children that also name their mother as Elsey. Notice that his last daughter Alice Elsey was likely named for her mother, and this would probably not have happened if he was married to Mary Webb in 1707. These birth records are important to keep in mind when, in Chapter Four, I explore a mystery line of Perrigos.

The reason for Ezekiel's move to Piscataway, New Jersey, is not certain, but as discussed above, it may have been partially religion and the availability of land. He was certainly living there by 1695, as he married there and his children were born there. Piscataway is about 150 miles south of Saybrook and is now a suburb of New York City. The settlers in the Piscataway area in the early 1700s were primarily Baptists and Puritans moving from New Hampshire looking for land, so we can assume it was land needs that made the move necessary. I have records that associate Ezekiel with the Dutch Reformed Church in Connecticut, but I have seen no such records in New Jersey. He remained in Piscataway until his death in 1724, and his estate included what was described as the "family farm" in Saybrook. He probably inherited his father's land, as the 1719 court case involving that estate contained a statement that his only brother, Robert, received only one shilling in his inheritance. Having lived in this area, I can offer an observation that it was close to the coast. I have seen descriptions of the farmland of that area when settled. A farm might consist of sixty acres of real estate with fifty-seven acres of fine swamp. I suspect that to be the situation with the Perrigo farm. The land description in his will uses a swamp as a landmark, hence the title for this chapter. The swamp situation was not dealt with for several years. Hence Ezekiel sought land in New Jersey, and his brother Robert Jr. went to Boston. Ezekiel inherited the swamp, but it may not have been substantial enough to produce a living, thus motivating the move to New Jersey. This farm was later listed in Ezekiel's will in 1724.

Robert Perrigo Jr.

Born: 1661
Died: 16 January 1711, Boston, Massachusetts
Birthplace: Saybrook/Lyme, Connecticut
Married: Around 1686 to Mary (last name unknown)
Buried: Unknown location, probably in Boston, Massachusetts

Robert is the son of Robert Perrigo Sr. and Sarah Elizabeth Smart of Lyme, Connecticut. I added the suffix Jr. to aid in understanding the story, but I found no evidence he used this suffix. As we do not have his birth records, his birth year was computed from his Boston death records that gave his age. His father's 1719 estate case summons did not list him as an interested party with his brother and cousins, as he was dead by 1711, but he was accounted for in a written summary of that court case. Robert Jr. apparently received only one shilling from his father. The Cutter Account also is supportive of his father being Robert.

He married Mary (last name unknown) around 1686 in Lyme, Connecticut, where his son John was born in 1698, and Ezekiel in 1701. A 1699 Connecticut Middlesex County census shows he lived there that year. The family then moved to Raynham, Massachusetts, where his son James was born in 1702.

We have the records reflecting his service in the British Army from 1703 to 1704 for forty-four weeks in Queen Anne's War. These records are recorded in *Massachusetts Officers and Soldiers, 1702–1722: Queen Anne's War to Dummer's War*, listed in the Reference Section below. Those records indicate he served in an expedition to Canada. He was likely already living in Massachusetts by the time of his service, as son James was born there in 1702. There were no English draft or conscription laws in the early 1700s, and one can imagine that the Perrigo brothers (Ezekiel and Robert Jr.) did not feel a strong patriotic urge to serve their country. It was the money pure and simple. Their father, while not wealthy, was a mariner and probably lived a comfortable life from a financial perspective. I believe that second-generation Ezekiel and Robert Jr. did not enjoy that level of comfort. They served for the cash, as you will see with their sons and the French and Indian War later in the book. He lived in Boston in 1710 and was renting his home from a Mr. Isaac Royal. I have that rent receipt.

On 14 July 1704, Robert Jr. conveyed about twenty acres of land to Joseph Peck of Lyme. This land was on the Beaver River and may have been a grant he had received from the town (Lyme Land Records (original) 1-58, 83 and Saybrook Land Records (original) 1-25). Remember, while his brother and sisters inherited land, Robert did not. I found additional Saybrook and Lyme land transactions between other Perrigo family members and the attorney Joseph Peck for land in 1705. These transactions probably involved land Robert Perrigo Sr. left to his children Sarah Perrigo Royce and Hannah Perrigo Creese. I found no transactions for Mary Perrigo Downing, sister to Sarah and Hannah, so she either retained her inheritance or sold it at another time. Their stories follow below.

Robert Jr. died in Boston, Massachusetts, and his will was proven in Saybrook, Connecticut. I have the Boston Vital Records of 1622–1982 that record his death at the age of fifty years old. We can speculate that his will was filed in Saybrook and needed to be proven and executed in that state and court jurisdiction.

His children were:
- John, 1698–1783. Revolutionary War Patriot. Remained in Boston.
- Ezekiel, 1701–1779. Remained in Boston.
- James, 1702–1786. Revolutionary War Patriot and my sixth great-grandfather.

It is important to mention that his son Ezekiel was born and lived nearly his entire life in Massachusetts and should not be confused with the second-generation Ezekiel discussed above. This Ezekiel, who was married three times, will be discussed later in the book.

Sarah Perrigo Royce (Royse)

Born: 9 November 1663

Died: 3 November 1728, Mansfield, Hartford County, Connecticut (Current Tolland County)

Birthplace: Saybrook, Middlesex, Connecticut

Married: 29 November 1683 to Sergeant John Royce in New London, Connecticut

Buried: Probably Old Mansfield Cemetery in Mansfield with her husband

She was the second-generation daughter of Robert Perrigo Sr. and Sarah Elizabeth Smart of Saybrook, Connecticut. She married Sergeant John Royce (Royse) (1663–1724) of Hartford, Connecticut, at the age of twenty years old. John was the son of Jonathan Royce and Deborah Woodward of Hartford. His father later became a city official in Ipswich, Massachusetts. Sarah and her husband are listed in her father's probate court case summons of 1711, as well as in the Cutter Account.

I found at least three spellings for this family name on official documents: Royce, Royse, and Roys. Royce was the spelling on several official documents and the tombstone.

John was a landowner and businessman and was one of the founders of Windham, Connecticut. After attending the first meeting of founders in 1692, in which he was appointed the town surveyor, he served in several official capacities for the town, including selectman. (Source: *History of Windham County, Connecticut* by Richard M. Bayles, shown in the Reference Section.) In 1702, after the birth of his seventh child, the Royce family moved to Mansfield, Connecticut, where they remained until his death. Other researchers have shown that he owned land in Mansfield well prior to his living in Windham, and that he served as a selectman in Mansfield from 1710 to 1717. By 1715, he also served as a representative to the Connecticut General Assembly in New Haven.

John likely served in one or more local militias, as some public records reflect that rank, as does his tombstone. John is buried in the Old Mansfield Center Cemetery in Mansfield.

John and Sarah had the following eleven children:

- John, 23 July 1686–11 December 1699
- Moses, 6 June 1689–30 July 1768
- James, 13 August 1691–6 January 1766
- Patience Arnold, 4 September 1698 – Unknown death date
- Aaron, 17 February 1695–Unknown death date
- Daniel, 27 May ? –Unknown death date
- Ebenezer, 31 March 1699–before 21 July 1743
- Dorothy Cross/Turner, 14 February 1701–Unknown death date
- David, 28 May 1703–28 March 1759
- Benjamin, 9 November 1706–Unknown death date
- Patina, ca. 1710–Unknown death date

Hannah (Anna) Creese

Born: 31 March 1674

Died: Unknown death date, but probably prior to 1729 in Cape May, New Jersey

Birthplace: Lyme, New London, Connecticut

Married: 17 July 1693, Lyme, New London, Connecticut to John Creese

Buried: Unknown location, but probably Cape May, New Jersey

Hannah is the second-generation daughter of Robert Perrigo Sr. and Mary Marah Wood of Lyme, Connecticut. Her birth is listed in the Lyme birth records as their child with the given birth date. She and her husband are also listed on the 1719 summons pertaining to her father's probate case as well as being mentioned as a daughter of Robert in the Cutter Account.

I found few original records documenting her life beyond her birth records and the court summons mentioned above; however, her husband's will of 1729 contains the names of their children, one being named Hannah. This will does not mention his wife Hannah, so it is possible that she was dead by 1729. John's death records indicate he was married, so either Hannah was still living, or he had remarried. The 1705 land transactions mentioned above involving land inherited from her father seem to document that her husband was John Creese and that she was the daughter of Robert Perrigo Sr.

John was a yeoman. This title merely indicates he was a British, non-slave-holding farmer. I found records that his father, Arthur, and his siblings moved from New York to Cape May and all owned land in what was to become an early American tourist location. It remains a popular destination to the present. I believe all their children were born there. Cape May is located on the New Jersey peninsula.

Their children were:

- Robert, 1690–1768
- John Jr., 1691–1788
- Eunice Somers, 1692–1744
- Comfort Steelman, 1705–Unknown death date
- Hannah, Unknown birth and death dates
- Penelope, Unknown birth and death dates
- Josiah, 1717–1758

Although the birth and death dates for Hannah and Penelope are unknown, they were listed in their father's will, and Josiah was mentioned as less than twenty years old; therefore, I assumed that both Hannah and Penelope were older than Josiah in this listing.

Mary Downing
Born: 1 April 1677
Died: 3 November 1737, New Groton, Middlesex, Massachusetts
Birthplace: Lyme, New London, Connecticut
Married: August 1697 in Groton, New London, Connecticut, to Jonathan Downing
Buried: Unknown location

Mary was a second-generation Perrigo and the daughter of Robert Perrigo Sr. and Mary Marah Wood of Lyme, New London, Connecticut. As with her sister Hannah, we have her birth records recorded in Lyme and other published birth records. The primary source for her later life is provided by the court summons of 1719 for her father's probate case. She is shown in that summons as is her husband, Jonathan Downing. They were shown to be living in New London, Connecticut, at that time.

Her husband, Jonathan (1677–1729), was the son of John Downing and Mary Bunce of Groton, Connecticut. Although few records were found, I believe they were married in August 1697 in New London, Connecticut. Jonathan and Mary were members of the Church of England of New London, and records exist for their marriage and the birth of their son Jonathan (Jr.). I found few records for their subsequent children, but Jonathan's will lists their names, which are also provided by other researchers. Those children were:

- Mary, 1699–1761
- Jonathan Jr., 1703–1786
- Elizabeth, 1705–1718
- Christopher, 1719–Unknown
- Nathaniel, 1721–1766
- Joseph, 1723–Unknown
- Jedediah, 1725–1750
- Perigo, 1726–1782. This spelling is from the will.

The Downings spent their married lives in and around Groton, Connecticut. As a matter of note, other researchers have documented this Jonathan Downing marrying Elizabeth Perrigo, sister of Mary. That would not have been possible, as Elizabeth did not live to adulthood. It is my belief that Jonathan and Mary's daughter Elizabeth Downing was being confused with Mary's sister, but that is speculation. It is also interesting to note that their daughter Elizabeth was possibly named after Mary's recently departed sister and that they named their youngest son Perigo.

Abigail Perrigo

Born: 3 July 1681

Died: 1683 in Groton, Connecticut

Birthplace: Lyme, New London, Connecticut

Married: Never married

Buried: Unknown location, probably in New London, Connecticut

Abigail was a second-generation Perrigo and daughter of Robert Perrigo Sr. and Mary Mariah Woods of Lyme, New London, Connecticut. Her birth date and parents are recorded in the Lyme Vital Records, of which I have a copy. Abigail probably died as an infant, possibly by 1683. She is not listed in the probate summons case discussed above, so she was certainly not alive by 1719. Little else is known of her.

Elizabeth Perrigo

Born: 30 October 1683

Died: 1693 in New London, Connecticut

Birthplace: Lyme, New London, Connecticut

Married: Never married

Buried: Unknown location, probably in New London, Connecticut

Elizabeth was the second-generation daughter of Robert Perrigo Sr. and Mary Mariah Woods of Lyme, Connecticut. As with the other Robert Perrigo children, we have her birth records from the city of Lyme, Connecticut. Little else is known of Elizabeth except that, in the interpreted notes with her father's probate case summons, she was noted as being dead by 1693.

Chapter Four

"Witches and Baptists Need Not Apply"

Generation Three

Thomas Perrigo

Born: 16 April 1699

Died: After 1724 in Woodbridge, Middlesex County, New Jersey

Birthplace: Saybrook/Lyme, Connecticut

Married: Unknown

Buried: Unknown location

Thomas was the third-generation son of Ezekiel Perrigo and Allice or Mary Webb and was born in Piscataway, New Jersey. He is shown as a son on his father's will of 1724, and his birth is also shown in New Jersey Births and Christenings 1660–1890. We have been unable to document a marriage; however, we believe he had a son who was born in New Jersey. I am uncertain of Thomas's date of death except that he was alive at the time his father wrote his will in 1724 and was still alive at the time of his son's birth in 1745. His proposed son is:

- Joseph Perrigo, 1745–1840

His son is an unproven relationship that will be discussed at length in the Joseph Perrigo section in Chapter Four. Others have held the belief that this Joseph was the son of David discussed next, but I believe that Joseph was born in New Jersey and David lived his married life in Massachusetts. The death dates of David and his wife and the birth dates of their well-documented children seem to preclude David as being his father.

Beginning with David Perrigo below, we will see generations three, four, and five, members of the Perrigo family being born in Massachusetts. The Figure 8 map in Chapter Five depicts the Massachusetts Counties. This map will be useful as we explore where the various family groups lived for more than one hundred years.

David Perrigo

Born: 29 August 1701

Died: 1746 in Boston, Middlesex, Massachusetts

Birthplace: Piscataway, Middlesex, New Jersey

Married: 24 December 1735 to Katherine (Catherine) Alsop (1715–1745)

Buried: Unknown location

David is a third-generation Perrigo and was a son of Ezekiel Perrigo and Allice Else. As was discussed earlier, the name of his mother is not certain, but it is likely Elsey. He is listed in his father's 1724 will. The Cutter Account also supports this relationship, and his birth location is consistent with the location of his father at the time of his birth. We emphasize this connection because of the several other David Perrigos (five) of this line and the fact that published references get them confused. The Perrigo Papers by Robert Bishop may not have made this distinction clear, and the Cutter Account is also not clear on the relationships of the several Davids. I also discovered some additional Davids, and I will attempt to assign them all to the correct family groups in this project.

We have not found many sources pertaining to his life in New Jersey and later life in Massachusetts, except two court documents attesting to his appearance in New Jersey and Massachusetts courts on routine matters. It appears that he lived in Massachusetts after marriage to Catherine in 1735, and we have those Boston Town marriage records. I have seen statements made by other researchers claiming that David Jr.'s mother was Elizabeth Dening and that she filed a paternity suit, but I do not have those court documents. We can find no references to that marriage if there was one. His marriage to Catherine Alsop (1715–1745) is proven, and they had the following four children:

- Abigail Fouseur, 1735–1760. Born in Gloucester.
- John Kemp, 1735–1757. Killed in the French and Indian War.
- David Jr., 1736–1780. Born in Gloucester.
- Rachael, 1741–Unknown. Born in Gloucester.

David was sued for eleven pounds in Bristol, Massachusetts, in February 1743 for a debt owed to Eric Richmond. Notice that his wife, Catherine, died in 1745 and that David died in 1746 at about the age of forty-five. Their children were all less than ten years of age when orphaned.

As shown by the birth of three of their children, he lived in Gloucester in Essex County until 1741. Gloucester is a north shore community town. Rachael's birth is proven in that town. I have been unable to prove his death location of Middlesex County, which is adjacent to and west of Essex County, so he possibly moved between 1741 and his death in 1746.

It is important at this point to discuss claims made by both Robert Bishop and the Cutter Account that Joseph Hewes Perrigo was the son of David and Catherine. I believe the Joseph Hewes mentioned in their accounts never used the middle name of Hewes. Secondly, the only Joseph Perrigo of the fourth generation was the son of Thomas Perrigo discussed above, and he was born in New Jersey and spent his entire life in that state. This fourth-generation Joseph was also not the father of the several Patriots of Pownal—namely David, Rufus, and Dr. John—as given in the Perrigo Papers. Those relationships will be developed in the next two chapters. I will mention there was a Joseph Hewes, but he was a fifth-generation family member and the son of Robert, who will be discussed later in this chapter. Simply put, David and Catherine did not have a son Joseph.

The Mystery New Jersey and Connecticut Line

Throughout the research of the third generation of the Perrigo line, I found at least three Perrigos from Connecticut records that seemed to not fit into any family group I had recorded. These individuals appeared to be father, son, and grandson starting in New Jersey and following with a son and grandson in Connecticut. The grandson was a Revolutionary War Patriot. I suspect that the first of this line was possibly the son of Ezekiel (1658–1724) of the second generation, discussed above. I will mention these three men and their families, recognizing that I am merely proposing this relationship as I cannot document the connection of this line to a known Perrigo line. They are not included in the family tree chart in Figure 3 for this reason.

John Perrigo
Born: 1695
Died: After 16 September 1783 in Boston, Middlesex, Massachusetts
Birthplace: Monmouth, New Jersey
Married: Hannah Prentice (1708–1786)
Buried: Unknown location

John is a possible third-generation son of Ezekiel Perrigo and Allice Elsey of New Jersey. This would make him a brother of Thomas and David discussed above in this third-generation chapter. While Thomas and David are listed in Ezekiel's will, John is not, and I have found no records supporting this relationship. The Piscataway birth records support both Thomas and David being sons of Ezekiel, but not John.

The discovery of this line adds further complexity and further confusion to the Perrigo genealogy because of the often-used given name of John. This John can easily be confused with John (son of Robert Jr.), who was born three years after the birth of this John. They are not the same man. Other researchers have attributed the middle name of Kemp to this John; however, I believe they have him confused with John Kemp, son of David Perrigo. The John Kemp Perrigo I have included in this project is mentioned in the will of second-generation Ezekiel Perrigo as a grandson, not son. In short, I can find little evidence proving the existence of this John Perrigo, except for the existence of his son William and grandson William the Patriot.

I discovered this line as I researched Revolutionary War Patriot William Perrigo (1756–1825) of Connecticut and later New York, who appears to be the son of William Perrigo (1734–1793), who might be the son of this John.

Ezekiel Perrigo

Born: 1701

Died: 1779 in Boston, Suffolk, Massachusetts

Birthplace: Boston, Suffolk, Massachusetts

Married: (1) Susanna Wilson 1725, (2) Sarah Farnham 1744, (3) Ann Wooster 1753

Buried: Unknown location, but probably in Boston, Massachusetts

Ezekiel is a third-generation Perrigo and is a son of Robert Perrigo Jr. and Mary. I establish this relationship based on the Cutter Account and the probate records of his wife Susanna Wilson's father. This document mentions Ezekiel and his brother John as sons-in-law. John married Susanna's sister Elizabeth Wilson. This is an important finding, as we see several researchers claiming this Ezekiel is the son of second-generation Ezekiel Perrigo, who was a son of Robert Sr., but that is not correct. He is the son of Robert Jr.

It is worth noting that Ezekiel and brother John probably owed their father-in-law money, as he directed in his will that whatever they owed him be taken out of their inheritance.

Ezekiel was married three times. First to Susanna Wilson in 1725 in Boston in a Presbyterian Church, and she died in 1744. He then married Sarah Farnham in December 1744, also in Boston. She lived until 1753, and he then married Ann Wooster in October 1753 in Falmouth, Maine. We have those marriage records and his children's birth and death records from the Old North Church of Baltimore. That church was an Anglican (Church of England) church, and it still stands and is a historical monument. The church is famous from its role in the ride of Paul Revere on 18 April 1775, four years before the death of Ezekiel. One wonders what role, if any, did Ezekiel play in that alert. Did he see the lanterns? Did he know Paul? The records of the Old North Church contain several entries concerning Ezekiel and his family, as well as his brother John and his family. We are left to wonder if they were neighbors and what they did for a living. I have found no records that answer those questions.

We believe Ezekiel had three children:

- Susanna, 1726–1729, died in infancy
- John, 1745–1749, died in infancy
- Judith, 1749–Unknown death date

The mother of Susanna was Susanna Wilson, and the mother of John and Judith was Sara Farnham. The location of Ezekiel's death is unknown. Possibly in Maine, but likely in Boston.

James Perrigo

Born: 1702

Died: 2 February 1786 in Pownal, Bennington, Vermont

Birthplace: Raynham, Bristol, Massachusetts

Married: Lydia Hayward in March 1727 or 1728 in Bridgewater, Plymouth, Massachusetts

Buried: Unknown location, but probably in Vermont

Service: Sixth Company of Colonel John Bailey's Continental Army Twenty-Sixth Regiment of Massachusetts. Later designated at the Second Massachusetts Regiment of the Continental Army.

Rank: Private

Service Dates: 10 April 1777–January 1778, with a break of AWOL

Lineage: His son David was the father of Justus J., and his son Justus Jr. was the father of Martin Vanburen, his son was Andrew Jackson, and his daughter was Blanche Francis Perrigo Adams, my grandmother. James would be my sixth great-grandfather.

DAR: None

SAR: None

James is a third-generation Perrigo and the son of Robert Perrigo Jr. and Mary, and he was born in Raynham, Bristol, Massachusetts. We know he is the son of Robert Jr. as he is mentioned with his brother Ezekiel in a court summons pertaining to his grandfather's estate in 1719. This document also gives his town of residence at that time. The Cutter Account also supports this relationship as do the Bishop Perrigo Papers. I could find no official records establishing his birth, with the exception that *The Record of Births, Marriages and Deaths in the Town of Stoughton*, listed in the references below, attributes the births of his sons and daughter to him and his wife Lydia. James is a great-grandfather to most of the current Missouri line of Perrigos, except for the New Jersey line I will discuss later in the book.

He married Lydia Hayward (1708–1791) on 4 March 1727 or 1728 in Bridgewater, Massachusetts. This marriage is documented in the Town of Stoughton records and Bridgewater records. He probably filed this marriage in his town of residence and Lydia's residence. This document is listed in the Reference Section below. This listing was an "intention to marry" entry, which was in 1727, with marriage in 1728.

Lydia was the daughter of Joseph Hayward Jr. and Sarah Crossman of Bridgewater. Lydia is listed as their daughter on page 73 of *The Brett Genealogy* listed in the Reference Section. I also have a copy of her Bridgewater birth records for 1708 listing her parents.

The Haywards were long-time citizens of Bridgewater and were landowners there. Her mother, Sarah, was the daughter of Joseph Crossman and Sarah Alden of Taunton and later Bridgewater. Sarah is a *Mayflower* Descendant, thus her daughter Lydia would be also. Her second great-grandfather,

John Alden, was a crewmember on the 1620 *Mayflower*, which would not automatically make him a *Mayflower* Descendant, but he chose to remain in the Colonies and thusly is recognized as a passenger. I suspect his choice was logical as he soon married Priscilla Sarah Mullins, who was a passenger on the ship with her family. Her father William and mother both died on the ship the winter after its arrival in Massachusetts. John was the seventh signer of the Mayflower Compact and was the last male survivor of those who came on the *Mayflower*.

I remember being taught in grade school that John's friend Miles Standish was interested in proposing to Priscilla, so he asked his friend John to inform Priscilla of his intentions. Her response according to William Webster was, "John, you should speak for yourself." That response apparently led to the following genealogy:

Parents of Lydia:
- Joseph Hayward Jr., 1673–1746
- Sarah Crossman, 1686–1746

Parents of Sarah Crossman:
- Joseph Crossman, 1659–1696
- Sarah Alden, 1685–1713

Parents of Sarah Alden:
- Joseph Blunden Alden, 1626–1697
- Mary Simmons, 1638–1697

Parents of Joseph Blunden Alden:
- John Alden, 1599–1687. *Mayflower* passenger, my tenth great-grandfather.
- Priscilla Mullens, 1602–1685. *Mayflower* passenger.

The references for the *Mayflower* passenger list are shown in the Reference Section of the book under *Mayflower* listing for Lydia Hayward and the Honorable John Alden. I will not list the proof of relationships for the Hayward, Crossman, and Alden families, but I have the birth, marriage, and probate records for the four generations of this well-researched family connecting Lydia to the Aldens.

The John Alden home of about 1630 still stands in Duxbury, Plymouth, Massachusetts, and is a national historical landmark. It is a ¾ Colonial-style home with two stories and has probably not changed much since he lived in it. I have included a photo of this home in Chapter Seven, Figure 11.

It is always interesting to consider the question, how did James Perrigo and Lydia Hayward meet? Her family had deep Pilgrim roots, and the Perrigo family was likely not known for religious fervor. I also suspect the Perrigos were not particularly wealthy, perhaps poor. James lived several miles away on the south side of Boston in Stoughton and Lydia in Plymouth County southeast of Boston. I present two thoughts for consideration in this question. First, James was born in Raynham, not far at all from Bridgewater. These towns are in different counties, but only about seven miles separate them. Secondly, the Haywards owned property in Taunton, south of Raynham, and would have likely passed through the town of Raynham on the way from Bridgewater to Taunton on the old "King's Highway."

I know of four sons and a daughter of James and Lydia:

- Robert, 1729–1808. Lived in Rhode Island and New York and was a Revolutionary War Patriot.
- James Jr., 1731–1808. Lived in Massachusetts and was a Revolutionary War Patriot.
- John, 1733–1811. Revolutionary War Patriot. Died in Chittenden, Vermont.
- Mary, 1737–1761. Died at the age of twenty-four in Killingly, Windham, Connecticut.
- David, 1738–1808. Father of Justus Jr., my fourth great-grandfather. Died in Chelsa, Vermont. He too was a Revolutionary War Patriot.

It is important at this point in the James Perrigo story to establish a residency timeline of James and Lydia as I have some questions concerning where the family lived at an important point of their lives, the period of 1739–1765. We will see below why it is important to know where they lived during this period. It is important to note that all these locations are not more than twenty-five miles separated, except for Pownal, Vermont.

James Perrigo Timeline

Date	Event	Location	Source
1702	Birth	Raynham/Bristol	City records
1719	Summons	Stoughton/Norfolk	Court documents
1728	Marriage	Bridgewater/Plymouth	City records
1729	Birth of son Robert	Stoughton/Norfolk	City records
1731	Birth of son James Jr.	Stoughton/Norfolk	City records
1733	Birth of son John	Stoughton/Norfolk	City records
1737	Birth of dau. Mary	Stoughton/Norfolk	City records
1738	Birth of son David	Unknown	None
1739	Warning Out	Bridgewater/Plymouth	City records
1754	Warning Out (Robert)	Bridgewater/Plymouth	City records
1760	Probate Witness	Bridgewater/Plymouth	Court records
1765	Colony Census	Pownal/Bennington	State records
1777	Military	Pownal/Bennington	National Archives

Notes for timeline:

It is worth noting that his birth in Bristol County is adjacent to Plymouth County and that Raynham is only about seven miles from Bridgewater in Plymouth County, the home of Lydia.

The 1719 summons for his grandfather's estate establishes he lived in Stoughton in 1719.

Married Lydia in Bridgewater, Plymouth County, Massachusetts, in 1728.

Son David possibly born in Bridgewater, Plymouth, Massachusetts, in 1738.

James was a witness to son Robert and Sarah Shorey's legacy case involving her inheritance from her father Miles Shorey in 1760. Robert and Sarah lived in Bristol County, so perhaps James lived nearby. He was born in Raynham, Bristol County. Perhaps they were safe from warning out in Raynham. More on that issue below.

James and Lydia and sons John and David were living in Pownal, Vermont, by 1765.

I have documents proving his birth location in Raynham, Bristol County, in 1702 and then his residence in Stoughton from as early as 1719 until 1737. Son David may have been born in Bridgewater in 1738. In March 1739, the entire family was warned out of Bridgewater, Plymouth, Massachusetts, the hometown of Lydia. I have been unable to document James and Lydia's location from 1739 in Bridgewater to Pownal in 1765, except that James seems to be in Bristol County in 1760 to witness his daughter-in-law's legacy case. It also interesting to note that son Robert and his wife were married in Plymouth, Massachusetts, in 1753 and then warned out in 1754. Robert soon moved to Rhode Island.

Records show James and his family were warned out of Bridgewater, Plymouth County, Massachusetts, in March 1739 by the constable. This ruling is based on a previous English practice in which a town would advise a poor transient person or family that the town was financially unable to provide relief for the poor. It was a mechanism for denying residency to the person or persons involved. It was English law that towns provide support to persons in need, therefore the town leadership "selectmen" would determine if the town could financially support additional poor arrivals and then order the constable to warn the new arrivals of the situation. See Figure 7 below for a copy of the warning document.

The book *Warning Out in New England*, listed in the Reference Section, gives some detail on the need for this practice and the supporting legislation in several New England colonies and towns. On 5 January 1739, an act was passed in Massachusetts establishing that citizens were not eligible for financial support even if they had paid taxes in that town (page 52). I think this legislation probably motivated the Bridgewater Selectmen to warn out families and individuals they had failed to warn out in the past. Perhaps the James Perrigo family was not destitute, but just poor, and the town needed to ensure they did not become a burden. The fact remains: when you were warned out of town, you left, and James Perrigo and family did just that.

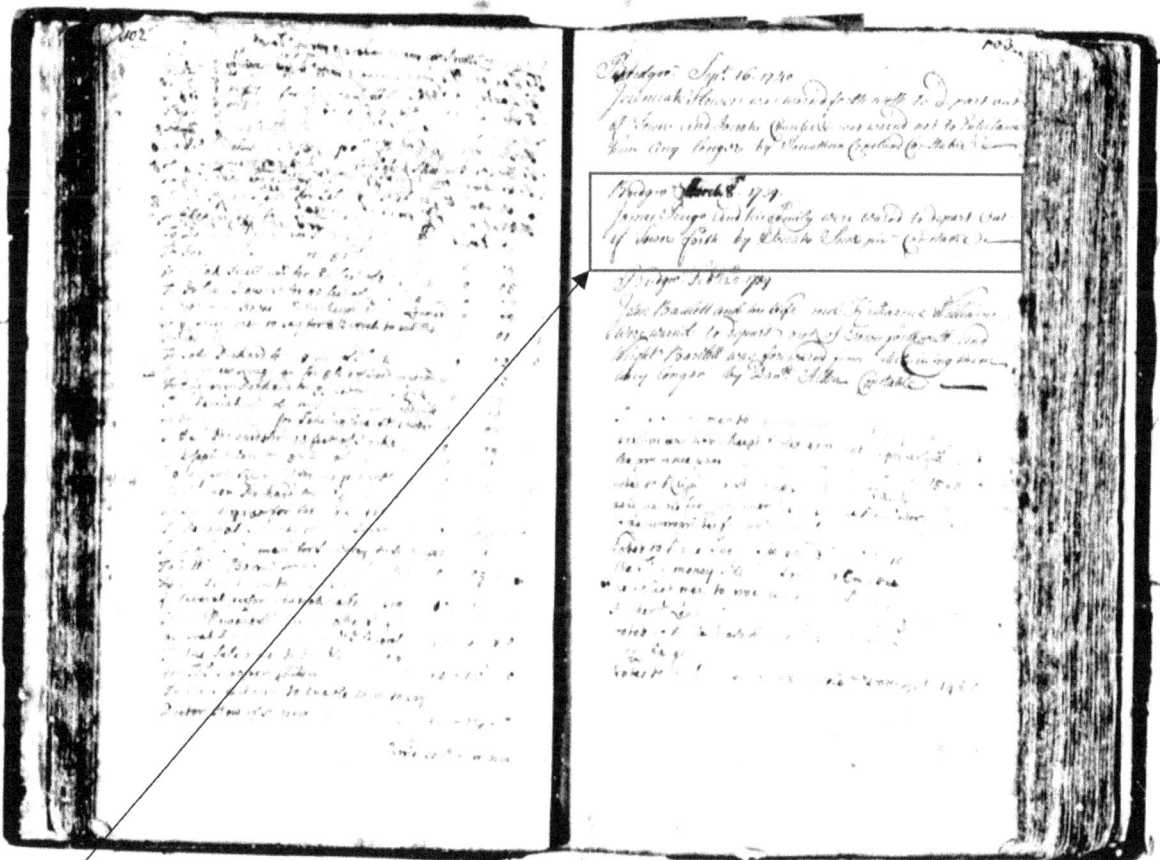

March 8, 1739. James Perrigo and his family were warned to depart out of town forth(wright) by Dansk Chapman Constable.

FIGURE 7: Massachusetts U.S. Town and Vital Records,
Bridgewater, Plymouth, Massachusetts, 1620-1988

Stoughton was settled in 1713 and incorporated in 1726, two years before their marriage. It was named after William Stoughton, who was the chief justice of the Massachusetts Colonial Courts and was a strong supporter of the Salem witch trials. David Thomas Vosel wrote an early history of Stoughton and "Historic Canton." Canton was part of Stoughton until 1797, when it was split into another town. He stated that in 1727 Stoughton had a population of 182 with 121 houses and 763 cattle and horses. The economy was based on six or seven sawmills, two grist mills, and four iron works. The Neponset River provided excellent waterpower for those industries. By 1769, the population was given as 2,100 citizens. Given the importance of early industry in Stoughton, we must consider that James worked in one of those mills. I doubt if he was a farmer, and given what happened next, I will rule that occupation out.

It appears that James and his family experienced a financial setback in Stoughton in 1737 or 1738.

They left their home of several years and moved to Lydia's hometown and were quickly ordered to move on. This fact seems to explain why a man over sixty years old would soon move to the frontier in Vermont. They were probably more welcome there. Land grants were possible, and sons John and David had experienced the French and Indian War, seen New York, lived in New York briefly, and moved on to Pownal. What did he have to lose? The church information was taken from the Thomas Vosel book mentioned above. It also mentioned there was not a school in Stoughton until around 1739.

A mystery related to the financial setback discussed above is that I and other researchers have been unable to document the birth of their youngest son David. He seems to have been born at about the time of the turbulence from the possible financial difficulties and the warning out of Bridgewater. One must consider that registering the birth of a newborn required a trip to the city hall. If James was at all concerned about being vulnerable to warning out, then maybe he chose to skip this formality. That is a real possibility we are forced to consider. Remember, his first three children were not recorded by a church, but at the Stoughton City Hall. David was likely not born in Stoughton, or his birth would have almost certainly been recorded in that town. The only church in town until 1739 was the English Angelican Church, with Baptist and Catholic churches being established that year. None of the other family births were recorded in a church.

I cannot overlook this lack of documentation, because we have no other proof of relationship with his father and mother. His father did not leave a will. My research of the records of nearly every town in southern Massachusetts has not been fruitful. I am convinced that his birth was never recorded given the extensive research by myself and others.

These are the facts that seem to establish a father–son relationship, but this is not proof:

- David and brother Robert were hired to serve in the French and Indian War at the same time in the same unit. The documentation for this service used the term "hired" as opposed to enlisted.
- David and his father were counted in the Pownal Vermont 1771 census which established their residency in that town in 1765. I believe they were the first Perrigos to settle there as brother John arrived there one or two years later.
- David and his father signed a petition in Pownal at the same time.
- David and his father joined the same Massachusetts Revolutionary War unit. They enlisted in Massachusetts, but the town was four miles from Pownal.

My research of Revolutionary War Patriots over the years has revealed several respected historians claiming that nothing of consequence took place outside of Virginia during the Revolutionary War and immediately prior. While one should not discount the activities of Thomas Jefferson nor William Henry Lee's ability to persuade the Virginia House of Burgess to enact an early version of the Declaration of Independence, Massachusetts contributed to the beginnings of the revolution also. The Tea Party at

Boston was encouraged by Samuel Adams and did much to stir New Englanders to action. A lesser-known event also encouraged by Samuel Adams took place in Stoughton, the previous home of James and Lydia and their family. To be correct, James and Lydia were citizens of Pownal, Vermont, by the time of these activities, but their son James Jr. and his family certainly remained there after their departure. In fact, even though he lived in Wrentham, James Jr. joined a military unit in Stoughton early in the war.

The Stoughton Resolves were compiled at Doty's Tavern on 16 August 1774, and some historians hold that these Resolves were the basis for the Declaration of Independence, written the following year. This meeting included such notables as Rev. Samuel Dunbar and Paul Revere, and the location was chosen by Samuel Adams and Dr. Joseph Warren. Dr. Warren might not be a well-known name, but one can argue the revolution might not have been possible without his leadership. He was unfortunately soon killed in the Battle of Bunker Hill.

Why would a tavern be chosen as a meeting location? Meetings other than church services were prohibited, so Samuel Adams encouraged that this meeting be held a little farther from the coast than Boston. Doty's Tavern was a well-established meeting place with a reputation as a clean, well-run establishment often patronized by influential citizens. This location might not attract the unwanted attention of the British. The tavern was located on what was known as the Taunton King's Highway that linked Taunton with Boston.

The meeting resulted in a written resolve that was voted on and passed and eventually approved by the Continental Congress in Philadelphia at Carpenter's Hall on 17 September 1774. This story can be found in the article "Doty Tavern" by Daniel T.V. Huntoon, which is listed in the Reference Section of this book. The history of Stoughton was taken from Wikipedia.

I do not propose that James was involved in this important meeting, because I am certain he and Lydia were citizens of Pownal, Vermont by then, but I am convinced he was aware of it and the Resolves after the fact. One only needs to follow this story with the activities of three generations of the James Perrigo family to gain an appreciation for their desire for liberty and belonging to a community. They helped make history, and this meeting may have stirred their motivations to fight for their freedom. It is noteworthy that James Jr. had connections to Stoughton when this important meeting occurred, and he wasted no time in enlisting in the Continental Army when war began. He was already a member of the "minutemen." See the James Perrigo Jr. story in the next chapter.

We are uncertain of his arrival in Pownal, Vermont, but we see at least one petition signed by him there in 1776. We also have a Vermont 1771 census which establishes his presence in Pownal as early as 1765 along with his son David. That census is listed with the references below. He signed as a witness in his son Robert and his wife Sarah Shorey's legacy case in which she inherited from her father's estate. This was in 1760 in Bristol County, Massachusetts. These facts seem to date his movement from Massachusetts to Vermont between 1760 and 1765. It appears his sons John and David also moved to Vermont, while son Robert moved to Rhode Island and son James Jr. remained in Massachusetts.

He was a Patriot in the Revolutionary War in a Massachusetts regiment. This fact requires some explanation as he was a Vermont resident. *Massachusetts Soldiers and Sailors of the Revolutionary War* reports him as being from Pownal, Vermont. As a matter of note, I have seen his service reported as from Pownal, New York. That is explained by the fact that the New York colony claimed Vermont as a territory until the matter was settled by the first Continental Congress in 1791. It is also important to note that Massachusetts also claimed the Vermont territory.

We are left to ponder his livelihood in Pownal, as he signed a petition for land in that small town in 1887. He no doubt acquired land as a very early settler and may well have earned a living as a farmer. I have questioned the likelihood of Pownal being a farming region, but early descriptions of the land in and around Pownal describe the soil as being suitable for farming as opposed to land outside of Bennington County being rough and rocky. See the discussion of Pownal's early history above in Chapter Two.

James joined the Sixth Company of what I believe was the Twenty-Sixth Massachusetts Regiment of the Continental Army on 10 April 1777 at Williamstown, Massachusetts. This was just a few miles across the Vermont–Massachusetts state line. We have seen documents stating it was only four miles from Pownal to Williamstown. James had a short military career as he was reported absent without leave on 2 May of that year. We find him later in January 1778 in Captain Warner's company of the same regiment at Valley Forge. He was present for a muster that month, and it is unclear how much longer he served. The Massachusetts records do not mention the designation of the unit, but research has shown that Colonel Bailey commanded that unit, and it was probably in northern Massachusetts in April that year. This unit did see some important action, but its assignment to the Continental Army was changed to a state line unit and back again twice in 1777. It was, however, truly a Continental Line unit while at Valley Forge. While serving as a Continental Line unit, it was designated the Second Massachusetts Regiment of the Continental Army. It was commonly referred to as "Bailey's Regiment."

We should not be too quick to be harsh with the manner of his service, because he was not a young man. He was over seventy years old. This was not his son James Jr. who was in Massachusetts at that time, as we have his records of the Revolutionary War in another unit. Their military records clearly establish that they were different men. He was a landowner and his absence from the military from May to January might be explained by his farming responsibilities. We have the right man here, but he merely did what he could. Still a Patriot even if his records reflect he deserted. We should furthermore consider that James enlisted in a state militia that was soon reassigned as a Continental Line unit. This change would certainly result in the unit leaving Massachusetts, which is probably more than he had bargained for. It is also important to note that James rejoined his regiment at Valley Forge in December after being AWOL since April. His records do not reflect how long he remained at Valley Forge. His service is recorded in *Massachusetts Soldiers and Sailors of the Revolutionary War*, listed in the Reference Section.

His death date and location are uncertain. His wife Lydia died in 1791 in Stephentown, Rensselaer, New York.

John Perrigo

Born: 1698

Died: 1783 in Boston, Massachusetts

Birthplace: Lyme, New London, Connecticut

Married: Eliza or Elizabeth Wilson on 4 January 1729 in Roxbury, Suffolk, Massachusetts

Buried: Unknown location

Service: Served in the Revolutionary War

DAR: No

SAR: No

John is a third-generation Perrigo and a son of Robert Perrigo Jr. and Mary, and a brother to James above. He was born in Lyme, New London, Connecticut, and married Eliza or Elizabeth Wilson (1702–1783) in Roxbury, Suffolk, Massachusetts. He is named in his grandfather's estate court summons of 1717, as were his brothers Ezekiel and James. His wife was a sister of his brother James's wife and was mentioned in his father-in-law's will.

It appears that John, as with his brother Ezekiel, spent most of his adult life in Boston. He was born in Connecticut, as were his brothers James and Ezekiel, and married in Roxbury. His marriage is recorded in the Old North Church records. As discussed above in brother Ezekiel's story, that is a historical church. He can be found listed in the Boston tax assessor's list of 1780, but his address is not given.

I first considered the possibility that he served in the French and Indian War in Connecticut, but I believe the records I found belonged to his relative John Kemp Perrigo, also of Massachusetts. John Kemp was a fourth-generation Perrigo and will be discussed in the next chapter. This John would have been at least fifty-six years old for that war, but not too old to fight.

I have been forced to give serious consideration to the possibility that he was a Revolutionary War Patriot, having served in the Connecticut Third Regiment. I have his National Archives records. Again, his enlistment in a Connecticut regiment requires explanation. My research of this family line has not identified another John Perrigo of this generation who was located close to Connecticut except for the son of brother James. I must add that the mystery John Perrigo discussed above, possibly of New Jersey and later Connecticut, should be considered, but I can find little documentation of his existence in either location. The following paragraph seems to exclude the mystery John. If we quickly note that he was approaching his eightieth birthday, that would be correct. I have researched more than one eighty-year-old Patriot, and they existed—just go back a few paragraphs and read his brother James's story. Different unit but about the same age! Now read the next paragraph.

The Connecticut Third Regiment was initially a Massachusetts regiment that was approved for assignment to the Continental Line. This fact does not explain that a man of the age of John Perrigo was serving when he was not expected to do so. However, his records reflect that he served for only ten days in 1781 near the end of the war. After careful consideration, I will give John Patriot credit, as I have those records and simply cannot attribute that service to another John. He had no descendants, so no one has used his service for membership in either the DAR or SAR.

He and his wife Eliza or Elizabeth had no children. We found that in his will he left one-third of his assets to Susanna, the daughter of his brother Ezekiel. It is interesting to note that niece Susanna was dead by the time of his will execution; he had simply not updated his will. However, the will stipulated that the proceeds also be divided amongst her two children.

Chapter Five

"The Bridge to Nowhere Shall Not Be Built Here"

Generation Four

About Patriots

As I begin the history of generation four, it is appropriate to discuss the fact that three generations produced stories of Revolutionary War Patriots. I take this responsibility seriously, and I have been careful to not omit someone's story and equally careful to not grant this honor to an undeserving relative. I am not an amateur, having researched and documented more than five hundred Patriots for my forthcoming book *Beat Your Drum Loudly*. I have also taught related subjects to DAR chapters and other organizations for many years, and I have published an earlier book containing stories of more than twenty Patriots. That having been said, these stories are far from complete, and I am less than satisfied that I could not produce more in-depth reviews of these great men and their lives and contributions to this country. I plan to continue this quest.

An important part of a Patriot's story is their military organization and understanding how they might have fit into that unit. The basic military organization during the revolution was a regiment. That unit contained six to ten companies and would have been commanded by a colonel. A company might contain a hundred soldiers and was commanded by a captain. Soldiers were recruited by company and regimental commanders and often remained in a unit for their entire period of service; however, some soldiers might serve an initial enlistment then re-enlist in another unit. We find regiments being organized by cities, counties, and colonies, and they were usually so identified. The Continental Congress assigned quotas to all thirteen colonies to furnish regiments for Continental use, and these regiments were designated as Continental Line units. You will see Perrigo Patriots belonging in all these units. I make this important distinction in these stories. Some regiments served as colonial regiments and then were assigned as Continental Line units and then turned back to colonial control and back again. You will see that confusing fact play out later in the stories.

Not all Patriots were soldiers! Both the Daughters of the American Revolution (DAR) and the Sons of the American Revolution (SAR) assign Patriot status to those who performed other important duties, and I follow those guidelines. Some of those duties were:

- Elected officials who supported the revolution at city, county, colony, and federal level.
- Members of the various Committees for Safety. These organizations supervised the city and county militias. They put themselves at risk by performing these important duties and were vulnerable to activities of Loyalists and other misfits. Remember, this was as much a civil war as a revolution. Many would have been hung had they lost the war. They were not military and thusly would have received much different treatment than former military.
- Those individuals signing loyalty oaths required by many towns and counties. These records are available for the most part and would have surely been used by the British to exact retribution had they won the war.
- Individuals who sold or gave material support to the military organizations. This would include food for individuals or animals as well as boarding soldiers or providing them health care. Following the war, procedures were instituted to reimburse these individuals for this support at the county and state level. My second great-grandfather lost a musket to a local militia and later claimed that loss and was reimbursed. He would have been maybe ten or twelve years old. He did not serve in the military, and I believe his musket served in the Battle of Guilford Courthouse, but that is another story. Another group of people falling into this group is women. Their contributions to the revolution often go untold. Some sold supplies to local militias, or these supplies were just taken while their spouses were away with their units. Again, they placed themselves at risk of retribution from Loyalists for these acts. I have records of my sixth great-grandmother doing just that and later making a claim and being reimbursed following the war. Some women followed their husbands and units and performed important functions such as laundry and cooking. Few records exist supporting those activities, and these Patriots go unrecognized. I believe such a Patriot may be unrecognized in the Perrigo family, and I will discuss that question later.
- Those families that suffered deprivation. I have found one such example in Emma Jo's family line.

Here is how I documented the Patriots in this book. These references are noted in the Reference Section at the end of the book. I will always state the proof I have found to document service in the stories to follow.

1. Military records for most State and Continental Line units as well as for many local militias are retained by the National Archives. These records are readily available if they exist.

2. Some states published a list of soldiers from that colony who served. *Massachusetts Soldiers and Sailors of the Revolutionary War* is an excellent example. They are reliable references, but there may be several men with similar given names and surnames on those rosters.

3. Both the SAR and DAR have records of Patriots claimed by descendants for membership in those organizations. This is not proof of kin, and the lack of being listed in these databases does not prove they never served. I so note in this book those Perrigo Patriots with descendants using their service for membership claims. These files provide descendant records. Again, this is not proof of relationship, but they are useful, and I am grateful to both organizations for access to those records.

4. There are many published books and journals, sometimes written by regimental commanders, listing the names of their soldiers. Again, not proof of service, but they are very useful.

5. The state lists of pensioners that were produced following passing of the 1818 Pension Act and subsequent revisions. These records are official and signal that we should look closely for pension applications, which are very useful in gathering stories.

6. While not proof of service, I have newspaper accounts from the mid- to late 1800s mentioning a Revolutionary War Patriot.

7. Records of land grants and patents for military service. These official records attest to military service; however, I found few such records for Connecticut, Massachusetts, and Vermont.

8. Court records. I found one New York action filed by a Perrigo family member making a claim for reimbursement.

These references are only part of the documentation process. I expect to be able to place a Patriot candidate in a location at the time of enlistment that makes sense. Not necessarily the same colony, but it must make sense. You will see this occur with several Perrigo Patriots, and I believe I have it right.

Name spelling is an interesting part of the documentation process. If you cannot read or write well or at all, you are at the mercy of whoever is completing the paperwork. I found twenty-three different spellings for the family name of a sixth great-grandfather in my Patriots book. None were correct! This was not such a problem with Perrigo Patriots, as I believe most were quite literate and different spellings are easily explainable.

Once a Patriot is found, then the process begins to prove relationship. If I was unable to prove a relationship, I will so state in the story as well as why I believe we should claim them as kin. I will usually use the logic of "preponderance of evidence" in those instances.

Now the Fourth-Generation Stories

Joseph Perrigo

Born: 22 June 1745

Died: 1840 in New York, New York

Birthplace: Monmouth, New Jersey

Married: 1770 to Annie Platt

Buried: Unknown location

Service: None known

I have spent added attention in the research of this New Jersey Perrigo line for one important reason. There is a link to a new Missouri Perrigo line previously unknown to me. You will see this story develop in the next two chapters. It is important to note that most New England colonies conducted at least one census before the first U.S. census of 1790. New Jersey conducted three, but none survive. Accordingly, I have relied on tax and church records and published stories for much of my research of this family line. I previously discussed the problem with New Jersey marriage records of this era, and they are in limited supply.

Joseph is a fourth-generation Perrigo and son of Thomas Perrigo and an unknown mother of Piscataway, Middlesex County, New Jersey. This relationship differs from the family groups presented in the Bishop Perrigo Papers and the Cutter Account. The Perrigo Papers reported David Perrigo (1701–1746) as his father, which is also the relationship I reported for several years. Both David and Thomas were sons of Ezekiel and were New Jersey residents for several years. After close examination of the lives of brothers David and Thomas, it was apparent that David, who married in Massachusetts and lived there following his marriage for the remainder of his life, was not the father of Joseph, who seems to have spent his entire life in New Jersey. David's brother Thomas seems to be a more likely candidate as the father of Joseph. While the relationship of Thomas and David as sons of Ezekiel is proven, the relationship of Thomas to Joseph is not, or to David for that matter. In fairness to the Cutter Account, the claim is made that Thomas is either a son or nephew of Ezekiel. Furthermore, both David and his wife, Catherine Alsop, were dead by 1846, with Catherine having died in 1745. This fact seems problematic for Joseph being their son. I also have the birth records of David and Catherine Alsop's children in Massachusetts, and Joseph simply was not a son of David and Catherine Alsop for several reasons.

Joseph is reported to have been born in Monmouth County, New Jersey. I propose, and other documents support, that his father was Thomas, born in Piscataway, Middlesex County, only twenty or so miles from Monmouth, and they are adjoining counties. Ezekiel, father of Thomas, had lived in Piscataway since prior to 1700. These two counties are today suburbs of New York City, and in the 1700s this was the breadbasket for that city. New Jersey even today is called the "Garden State." It is likely that the New Jersey Perrigos were farmers.

A North American Family History account belonging to Family Search gives an account of Elizabeth (1792–1861), daughter of Joseph and Annie, as she married Joseph Stratton of Sussex County in 1807 and later moved to Ohio in 1817. This account states that Elizabeth's father, Joseph Perrigo, was a landowner and farmer in Sussex County prior to 1802. As Joseph and Annie were married in Middlesex County in 1770, they had apparently moved to Sussex County, the westernmost county of New Jersey, before 1802. In fact, it appears that their son Joseph M. was born in Sussex County in 1774, as were all their children after the birth of Joseph M. I also have an August 1781 Sussex County tax record showing Joseph as living there. The next paragraph further explains why I can place them in Sussex County.

Joseph and his immediate family were long-term members of the First Baptist Church of Wantage, Sussex, New Jersey. In the previous chapter, I related the story that this church and its members made a congregational move from Mansfield, Connecticut, to Newton Township of Sussex, New Jersey, by 1760. I do not mean that this family group made the group move to New Jersey, but it is likely that they were members of that church by the time of their marriage in 1770 as their children became members.

Joseph married Annie Platt (1750–1830) in New Jersey, and all their children were born there. The names and some information for their children were documented from the family bible of their son Abel, as well as from Sussex County church records. Three of the children presented were not listed in that family bible, as I so note. Joseph and Annie had the following eleven children, who will be discussed further in Chapter Six with the fifth generation.

- David, 1771–1850. Not listed in the family bible but remained in Sussex County. He is a Revolutionary War Patriot.
- Abel, 1773–1842. He remained in Sussex County.
- Joseph M., 1774–1864. Married in Sussex County, served in the War of 1812, and remained in New York City for the remainder of his life.
- James, 1776–1850. Moved to Guernsey, Ohio, and remained there.
- Isaac, 1782–1864. Married in New Jersey but died in New York City.
- William, 1784–Unknown death date. Little is known of him, and he is not listed in the family bible.
- Samuel, 1787–1830. Remained in Sussex County.
- Margaret Young, 1791–1843. Remained in Sussex County after marriage.
- Elizabeth Stratton, 1792–1851. Married in Sussex County in 1807 and moved via Pennsylvania to Ohio by 1817.
- Annie, 1794–Unknown death date. She is not listed in the family bible.
- Eleazer, 1799–1878. Moved to Wayne County, Ohio, and lived near his sister Elizabeth Stratton.

Source: Abel Perrigo family bible currently available from Greta Olsen or George Sweeney.

Family notes accompanying the family bible concerning the added names seem to base the reason for their addition on county census reports from 1830. I included those names for general information, and I must be clear that those relationships are unproven. As noted above, daughter Elizabeth married Joseph Stratton, the son of a Revolutionary War Patriot, and they soon departed New Jersey and moved across Pennsylvania to Ohio, where they were amongst some of the early settlers in that territory. There are some interesting stories in Ohio libraries about her life there. She was probably a tough and colorful pioneer.

As a matter of interest, Joseph and Annie's proposed son David was seemingly born in 1771 after his mother and father's marriage around 1770. I have found records attesting to the fact that he served in the Revolutionary War. Either his birth date is incorrect, or there was another David Perrigo of Sussex County, as he was not old enough for this war. This question bears further investigation.

Joseph's wife, Annie Platt, was the daughter of William and Catherine Platt. Annie was born in Great Budworth, Cheshire, England, on 13 January 1750, and she was twenty years old when they were married in New Jersey. I do not believe her parents accompanied her to America.

It is important to visit the fact that Robert Bishop believed that this Joseph Perrigo was the father to Rufus, David, and Dr. John Perrigo of Pownal. These fifth-generation men were Revolutionary War Patriots and will be discussed at length in Chapter Six of this book. I have proven these three Patriots were the sons of John Perrigo, who was a son of James Perrigo Sr., who will be discussed later in this chapter. I have been unable to associate this Joseph Perrigo with Pownal, Vermont at any point of his life, as he may well have spent his entire life in New Jersey, except for the period late in his life when he probably lived with a son in New York City. Mr. Bishop used the name of Joseph Hewes Perrigo in this instance, and I have found no evidence that he ever used that name. In fairness to Mr. Bishop, the Joseph Hewes of Pownal was old enough to be the father to these well-known Patriots, but the facts do not support that contention, and the Joseph Hewes referred to by Mr. Bishop was supposedly the son of David, which I also believe is not correct. He was the son of Thomas as discussed above. A professional researcher should quickly point out the fact that I have challenged an unproven fact with another. That is true, but until further evidence can be produced, I believe the logic of my claim should prevail as I am certain I have established the relationships of James Sr. and his sons of Pownal, and that alone clouds the long-held relationships of David and his supposed offspring. You will see this story unfold as we progress through this and subsequent generations.

I am uncertain of the death place of Joseph. I have records that establish that a person with this name died in New York City in 1846, and as at least two of his sons lived there at the time of his death, that is a reasonable claim.

While I have not adequately proven the relationship of Joseph with his proposed father Thomas, I am certain that available evidence establishes that he is not the Joseph Hewes Perrigo documented in the Cutter Account or the Perrigo Papers and that he is not the son of the second-generation David Perrigo (1701–1746).

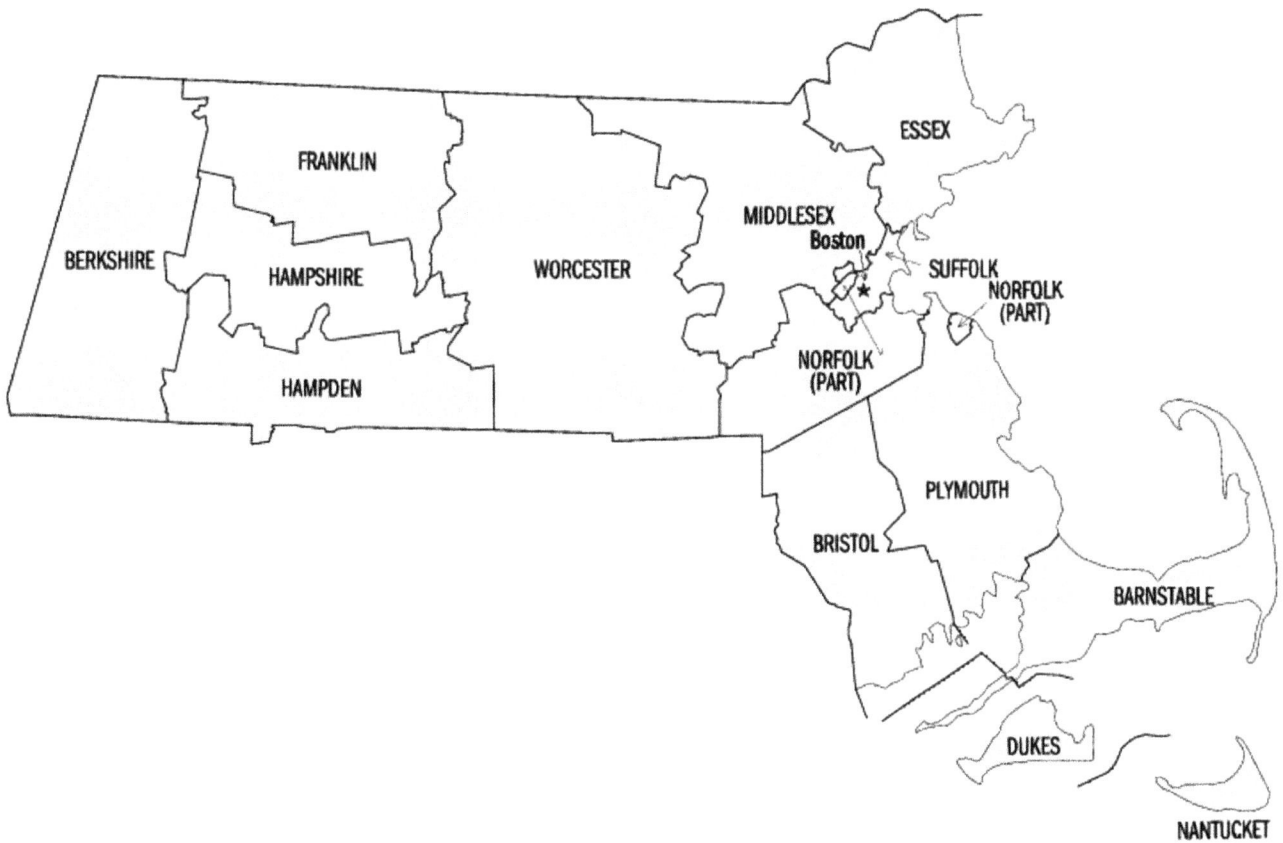

FIGURE 8: Massachusetts County Map.

Source: Wikimedia. See Reference Section below for credits.

John Kemp Perrigo

Born: After 1735

Died: 26 July 1757

Birthplace: Massachusetts

Married: Not known, but probably never married

Buried: Unknown location

I attribute the parentage of John to David Perrigo and Catherine Alsop. While this is an unproven relationship, he is mentioned in the will of his grandfather Ezekiel Perrigo, who listed him as a grandson. Ezekiel had two sons: Thomas and David. I believe Thomas had only one son, Joseph, discussed above, so his most likely parents were David and Catherine. John was orphaned after the death of Catherine in 1745 and David in 1746. I could find no evidence of caretakers after their death, but Uncles Ezekiel (1701–1779), James Sr. (1702–1786), and John (1698–1783) were close by. This connection may explain his next act.

He served in the Lyman Regiment in Connecticut, as did several other Perrigos during the French and Indian War. Again the question arises: Why was a Massachusetts man serving in a Connecticut unit? Incentives were offered to those serving, and that could explain the reason why several members of this family did so. I found records of many Massachusetts men serving in Connecticut. We found records listing his death date while serving with his regiment during the 1757 campaign. He was serving in New York at the time of his death at the age of twenty-two. I could find no further information about him until the French and Indian War in which he lost his life. A diary of another soldier of that unit reported that John was accidentally killed by another soldier who was cleaning his gun in a neighboring tent when it accidentally discharged. This event was described by Luke Gridley, and his diary is listed in the Reference Section.

The French and Indian War, if taught at all in school, is often portrayed as a single war led by Virginians under the command of Colonel George Washington, who was serving as a Virginia Militia officer. This conflict was much more than that. It was a series of campaigns funded by England and executed by various state militias, especially those of Connecticut. Their militias had been involved in a long-standing conflict with Native American tribes who were based outside the colony of Connecticut and would attack and retreat to New York. The Perrigo family originally settled in Lyme, Connecticut, by 1650 and was certainly threatened by Native Americans for more than one hundred years prior to the French and Indian War campaigns of the 1750s. I believe the family had multiple reasons to join in that fight. In fairness to the Native Americans, they had been treated quite unfairly by both the Pilgrims and Dutch settlers of Massachusetts and Connecticut for more than one hundred years. They had ample reason to fight for what had been taken from them.

David Perrigo Jr.

Born: 1736

Died: 9 May 1780 in North Yarmouth, Cumberland, Maine

Birthplace: Boston, Middlesex, Massachusetts

Married: 10 April 1757 to Abigail Brock in Gloucester, Essex County, Massachusetts

Buried: Unknown location

Service: Connecticut Militia in the French and Indian War

Service Dates: Fifteen days in 1757

David Jr. was the son of David Perrigo and Catherine Alsop of Boston, Middlesex, Massachusetts, and a fourth-generation Perrigo. Some researchers have listed Elizabeth Denning as his mother and asserted that she made a paternity claim in court, but I have been unable to prove that assertion. This David is the second David we document in this project, and he is not accounted for in the Cutter Account. Bob Bishop briefly discusses him in the Perrigo Papers as being a son of David and Catherine Alsop, which I believe to be correct. He goes on to discuss his belief that this David had a second wife, Susanna Varrel, and that they lived in Pownal. I do not find that to be correct, as the David of Pownal is proven to be a citizen of that town in 1765, while this David is in Massachusetts with Abigail Brock having children. The David who is husband of Susanna Varrel will be discussed later in this chapter. This David Jr. is clearly a distinctive family member and left records setting him apart from the five other David Perrigos of this line.

David married Abigail Brock (1736–1764) of Gloucester, Essex, Massachusetts. Her father was John Brock and her mother Abigail Ewell. John was a fisherman of that coastal town and was listed on the town "Poor List." I found several instances in which the town selectmen authorized payment for their medical and other expenses, culminating in the forced sale of their home to pay reimbursement to the city. We have the marriage records of David and Abigail, and they had seven children:

- Ezekiel, 1758–1803
- David III, 1760–Unknown death date
- Molly Tripp, 1763–Unknown death date
- John, 1764–1820
- Abigail, 1767–Unknown death date
- Elizabeth, 1771–Unknown death date
- Sarah, 1774–Unknown death date

The Gloucester Baptist Church birth records record the birth of his sons David III, Ezekiel, John, and daughters Molly, Abigail, and Sarah. These birth records clearly set him apart from David Perrigo of Pownal. I will note that I have added the suffix of III to this David to aid in our understanding of the several Davids in this line.

David Jr. served in the Fourth Regiment of the Connecticut Militia during the French and Indian War for fifteen days in 1757. He served under the command of Colonel David Wooster. We see several other Perrigo family members also serving, one losing his life. The question remains: Why Connecticut? First, Connecticut was not far from Boston. Second, Connecticut was the home colony for this family. Third, it was about the money. Cash, hard money, gold or silver, was in short supply in early New England. A two-week stint was no big deal, and it produced must-needed cash. As I discussed earlier, according to *History of Middlesex County*, Connecticut had long maintained a standing militia for the "French War," and this may have been seen as an opportunity for many young men to not only earn some cash but also get out of Boston. I will also repeat that I do not believe many men served only fifteen days in this war. Enlistments were commonly for a specific campaign, not a specific amount of time. These records I have used are an excerpt from other records. Few soldiers' entire records for the French and Indian War remain, so we are reliant on these excerpts. It is entirely reasonable to believe he served for more than fifteen days, but that proof is elusive. I found his service recorded in *Rolls of Connecticut Men in the French and Indian War, 1755–1762*, Volume II, listed in the Reference Section.

He was drowned in Cumberland, Maine, in June 1780. I have the post-mortem inquisition listing his name and that he drowned when he fell from a boat, and the conditions surrounding his death are not known. I have found no evidence of military service during the Revolutionary War, so it is possible that this was an employment-related accident. Perhaps he was logging, but that is speculation. Remember that the boundaries of Maine and Massachusetts were disputed until after the war, and he was probably working in pre-revolution Massachusetts at the time of the accident. The map in Figure 1 above highlights this problem, and he may not have been far from home at the time of the accident. Cumberland County is in southern Maine near the present-day Massachusetts and New Hampshire borders. There is a Cumberland City, but the referenced inquisition was a county responsibility. His home of Gloucester, Massachusetts, was a northern coastal town and was adjacent to the disputed Massachusetts, New Hampshire, and Maine colony lines. (See Figure 1 above.)

We find no records of his life after 1780, so it is likely that this is the correct David Perrigo who was killed in 1780. The David Perrigo of Pownal lived at least twenty-eight additional years.

Robert Perrigo

Born: 18 April 1729
Died: 18 December 1808 in Kingsbury, Washington, New York
Birthplace: Stoughton, Norfolk, Massachusetts
Married: (1) Susannah Holmes in 1754 and (2) Sarah Shorey in 1760
Buried: Unknown location in New York
Service: Two enlistments in the French and Indian War and then the Revolutionary War in the Second Rhode Island Regiment
Service Dates: Fifteen days in 1758 and fifteen days in 1762. At least three months ending in September 1780.

Robert is a fourth-generation Perrigo and the son of James Perrigo and Lydia Hayward. Stoughton, Norfolk County, Massachusetts, city birth records prove this relationship. His brothers James Jr., John, and David are all Revolutionary War Patriots.

Robert was born and married in Massachusetts. Stoughton is located about seventeen miles from Boston and thirty miles from Providence, so he did not stray far from this area until later in his life. His first wife, Susannah, died the year of their marriage in 1754 in Plymouth, Massachusetts, which is just south of Boston. We have records of his being warned out of Plymouth, Massachusetts, also in 1754. As with his father in Bridgeport in 1739, the warning out practice was notice that public assistance was not available. It was time to move on. He then married Sarah Shorey in 1760 in Bristol, Massachusetts. It is fair to say this area was settled by those seeking religious freedom, and history is filled with stories of those who wanted to practice a pure religion. It was hard to fit in if you were not an ardent and strict religious follower. We are not sure how the Perrigo family fit into this community that supported religious freedom only as long as it was of the correct variety. Salem was just on the other side of the town, and it was only sixty years since the witch trials there. As in the earlier chapter "Witches and Baptists Need Not Apply," if you were warned out of town, it was time to leave on a good horse.

I found records that Robert and his new wife, Sarah, received a legacy "inheritance" from her father's estate in November 1760. Her father's name was Miles Shorey. This court transaction was witnessed by his father, James, who may have lived near, as he moved to Pownal by 1765. James's location in 1760 is useful for discussions concerning his descendants James Jr. and James III later in the book. It is also useful in determining where his father lived after being warned out of Bridgewater in Plymouth County in 1739.

We find Robert in Providence, Rhode Island, in 1765 and 1766 operating a shop where he served as a "cordwainer." A cordwainer makes shoes from new leather as opposed to a cobbler that must rely on previously used leather. His shop was identified by the "sign of a boot," and he also sold butter in small amounts. It is likely that his shop was in Newport, but I found two distinct records attributing a boot shop to him, one in Providence and one in Newport. Having lived in Newport, I can relate that, while these towns are near to each other, Newport is located on Aquidneck Island. They are separated by Narraganset Bay, and there were no bridges in the 1700s. A trip between these towns would not have been a daily trip for a busy cordwainer, so we are left to wonder about his shops and if there were one or two. What is clear is that he had come a long way from being warned out of Plymouth, Massachusetts, just a few years earlier and thirty miles down the road. This information was provided by Oscar Perrigo of New York, who documented this occupation from *Rhode Island Historical Tracts* No. 15, p. 214.

He served in the French and Indian War in Connecticut in 1758, serving for fifteen days in the company commanded by Captain and later Colonel Wooster. Then again in 1762 he served as a sergeant in the Rhode Island Army in the French and Indian War in Captain Hawkins's Company.

He served in the French and Indian War in 1758 with his brother David Perrigo Jr., discussed above. As I have already mentioned, the fifteen days of service is in question, as with this instance, he was listed as being hospitalized in New York. He had apparently been wounded or was suffering illness.

He remained in Rhode Island, and we again find him in the Second Company of the Second Rhode Island Militia Regiment in the Revolutionary War. He served at least three and a half months in 1779. This was a local militia, so it probably saw little action, but one should not underestimate the importance of local security in this area, being just a few miles from Boston and near the main north–south business corridor from Boston to New York. This was a strategically important piece of real estate, and equally important waterways surrounded them. It was a hotbed of activity, and I have read accounts of city selectmen and safety committees as they discussed the importance of security in the area. Robert was likely more interested in the security of his family and business than earning a little cash, as was probably his priority during the French and Indian War ten years prior to the Revolution.

Robert moved to New York possibly around 1782, about the time his brothers and cousins moved there following the Revolutionary War. His son Dr. Robert Jr. later served as an officer in the New York Militia in the War of 1812.

He had two children by his second wife, Sarah Shorey:

- Joseph Hewes, 1763–1843. Patriot of the Revolutionary War.
- Dr. Robert Jr., 1765–1829. Patriot of the Revolutionary War and the War of 1812.

Robert died on 18 December 1808 in Kingsbury, Washington, New York.

James Perrigo Jr.
Born: 27 April 1731
Died: 20 December 1808 in Norfolk, Massachusetts
Birthplace: Stoughton, Norfolk, Massachusetts
Married: (1) Elizabeth Dickerman on September 1756 in Massachusetts, who died in 1767, and (2) Elizabeth Petee in 1758 who died in 1798 and (3) Thankful Wright in 1799, also in Norfolk, Massachusetts
Buried in the old Norfolk County Cemetery, Norfolk, Massachusetts
Service: He served in the French and Indian War in Massachusetts with his brother John. He also served with Colonel Marshall's Regiment in the Massachusetts Second Regiment under Captain Fisher in the Revolutionary War.
DAR: A 089021
SAR: P-268708

The book *The Record of Births, Marriages and Deaths and Intentions of Marriage in the Town of Stoughton from 1727 to 1845*, shown in the Reference Section, establishes his parents as James Perrigo and Lydia Hayward of Stoughton, Massachusetts, so he is a fourth-generation Perrigo. We believe he spent his entire life in Massachusetts, although the Perrigo Papers mistakenly place him in Pownal, Vermont, by 1790. It was actually his father who had moved to Pownal, probably by 1765. We see his father in a 1771 Vermont census that establishes his being there by 1765. It is reasonable to assume the son would migrate to unsettled territory and the father remain in the hometown, but that was not the case in this instance. The "Old Man" moved to the frontier. This reference also lists James Jr.'s intention to marry Elizabeth Dickerman.

He was a clockmaker in Wrentham, and a picture of one of his clocks is shown below in Figure 9. These clocks are truly works of art and are sometimes sold in modern antique auctions for high prices. He is recognized as possibly the first Massachusetts clockmaker. He was also a member of the Masonic lodge. I have a copy of his membership card.

FIGURE 9: James Perrigo Jr. Clock

His early clocks were constructed of wood works with painted faces and cabinets made by other craftsmen. As a matter of note, pictures of a clock made by his son James III are shown later in Figure 10 with James III's story. A close observer should note that the above clock face, although very similar to that in Figure 10, is attributed to J. Perrigo, not James Jr. Our logic to this issue is that James III discussed below generated records showing his name as James Jr. For some unknown reason, both James Jr. and James III did not recognize James Sr. Both James Jr. and James III held clockmaker licenses in Massachusetts. This situation is not unusual in genealogy research. There were in fact three James Perrigos from Norfolk County, Massachusetts, and the records establish them as father, son, and grandson, even if they did not use the correct suffixes to their names. Two made clocks, and one did not.

James Jr. served as a sergeant in the French and Indian War in Massachusetts, with his brother John in Thatcher's Regiment. The records reflect he was from Plymouth, Massachusetts. I think this Plymouth, Massachusetts, location may be a hint that his father and family remained in Plymouth County somehow after being warned out of Bridgewater. The time served during this enlistment is not certain, as men enlisted for campaigns, not necessarily for a set period. Thatcher's Regiment was assigned to the Crown Point and the Bay of Fundy expeditions. They likely served some of their enlistments in New York and probably saw some action. They did get to see New York, with John possibly remaining or returning after his service. Their records of service are contained in *Massachusetts Officers and Soldiers in the French and Indian Wars 1755–1756*, listed in the Reference Section.

James paid Ebeneezer Howe to serve on 19 April 1776 for ten and a half days for a minuteman call up. I first thought this record should be attributed to his son James III, but he was only two years old. This call up on 19 April was for the Battle of Lexington, the first battle of the Revolutionary War.

He later enlisted in the Massachusetts Second Regiment commanded by Colonel Marshall, and he served in Captain Smith's Company. The enlistment date was 27 January 1777, for three years. While it appears he remained in the same unit, the regiment was commanded by Colonel Reed Hawes, and his company was commanded by Captain Samuel Fisher when he was discharged in January 1780. His service is recorded in *Massachusetts Soldiers and Sailors of the Revolutionary War* listed in the Reference Section. I will mention that while the DAR has approved memberships based on his service, the unit attributed to his service differs from the above reference. It is important to discuss the fact that his brother John also served in the Second Massachusetts Regiment. That fact is a little confusing, as brother John's regiment was a Continental Line unit that was also designated as a state militia and then turned back to a Continental Line unit more than once. It was commanded by Colonel Bailey for most of the war. They were different units. I believe that James Jr. served his entire enlistment in the colony of Massachusetts. I have National Archives records supporting his service, but they are incomplete. The roster card reflects the Second Regiment but does not give the regimental commander's name. These records contain a single company roster but do not show the dates of service. The suggestion that there were two Massachusetts Second Regiments is not unusual. One was a Continental Line unit a few times as well as a state militia unit a few times. The Second Regiment to which James Jr. belonged was a Boston militia unit supervised by the Boston committee for safety. This duplication of units is common and occurred in Maryland and Virginia also.

He had a daughter with his wife Elizabeth Dickerman:
- Waitstill, 1759–1794

He had six children with his second wife, Elizabeth Pettee:
- John, 1774–1834 (Twin)
- James III, 1774–1834 (Twin)

- Jared, 1775–1865
- Molly Mann, 1777–1811 (Twin)
- Elizabeth "Betty," 1777–1805 (Twin)
- Robert, 1779–1834

His daughter Waitstill and son Robert were not listed in his will of 1805. Waitstill died in 1794, and we have her death records listing her father and mother. I have the birth records of Robert, but I am unsure why he was not listed in the will.

James Jr. died on 20 December 1808 at the age of seventy-seven. It is believed he is buried in the old Norfolk County Cemetery with his wife Elizabeth and daughter Waitstill, and my further research bears that contention to be true.

John Perrigo

Born: 1733

Died: 31 October 1811 in Essex, Chittenden, Vermont

Birthplace: Stoughton, Norfolk, Massachusetts

Married: 20 May 1728 to Mary (last name unknown, but possibly Flint)

Buried unknown location

Service: French and Indian War and the Revolutionary War

Service Dates: 1755–1756 in the French and Indian War. 11 to 21 October 1780 in the Revolutionary War.

DAR: A089023

SAR: P-268709

John was the son of James Perrigo Sr. and Lydia Hayward of Stoughton, Norfolk, Massachusetts. He was born in Stoughton, Massachusetts, where his parents had lived for several years before he relocated to New York and later Pownal, Vermont. His father was the son of Robert Perrigo Jr. (1661–1711), also of Massachusetts. We know father James was the son of Robert Jr. from court records involving a lawsuit over property in Massachusetts naming the children of Robert Jr. We know John was the son of James from several sources, including the Stoughton vital birth records and *Genealogical and Family History of Northern New York* by Richard Cutter, shown in the Reference Section.

I am unsure of the family name of his wife Mary, named in his 1805 will. I suspect that she might have been Mary Flint of New York, but that is not proven. Bob Bishop stated in the Perrigo Papers that David the drummer's mother was Mary Flint and David Perrigo the drummer was John's son. I must risk adding confusion to this family line by stating that Bob Bishop also claimed that David the drummer's father was Joseph Perrigo, and I have been unable to document that claim as John's will clearly establishes that he was the father of this David.

He enlisted in the Massachusetts Militia during the French and Indian War with his brother James Jr. under Captain Thomas Duty in the Thatcher Regiment. We have those records. See my description of that service above with the James Jr. story. I have always assumed that John returned to Stoughton, Massachusetts, after the war and later moved to Pownal. That assumption may have been wrong given that his sons David and Rufus made sworn statements for their military pension hearings that they were born in Dover, New York, in the late 1750s and early 1760s. Dover, New York, is across the New York and Connecticut state lines due north of New York City and in the Hudson River Valley. He probably got to see the valley in the 1755–56 enlistment and perhaps remained there. That may have been where the work was. He was, however, in Pownal by 1765. If Mary Flint was his wife, then he likely married in New York, as I have records of Mary Flint of New York and of her marriage to a Perrigo, but I have been unable to determine if her husband was John Perrigo.

John lived for a time in Pownal, Vermont, prior to and following the revolution as we see several petitions signed by him and sons David and Rufus. They were shown on the 1790 census there also.

During the revolution he served in the Vermont Militia under Captain Nathaniel Seely; the regiment was commanded by Colonel Samuel Herrick. Both the DAR and SAR recognize his service, and he did not live long enough to file for a pension for his Revolutionary War service. His service was for just ten days in October 1780 and is recorded in the National Archives as well as the *State of Vermont Rolls of the Soldiers of the Revolutionary War 1775–1783*, which is listed in the Reference Section. Colonel Herrick's regiment of militia was a large regiment whose purpose was local security within the southeast section of the state, including Pownal. While they probably saw no heavy combat, they did have combat losses and performed an important role. The regiment consisted of several basic infantry companies as well as at least one company of Rangers. Most of these companies were called up as needed, sometimes for only ten or twenty days, as was the case with this call up. I noticed that at least three companies were called up on 10 October, so the safety committee must have seen a threat in that area. He was paid for seventy miles of travel, so the threat must have been within a thirty-five-mile radius of Pownal.

We found that in Vermont prior to the revolution, he sold land to a man named Beloved Carpenter and held a note for thirty-three pounds for that debt. In 1776, Carpenter joined the King's Army, and the colony quickly confiscated that land. In October 1779, John requested that he be reimbursed for his loss from that confiscation, as Beloved Carpenter still owed John for the land. He submitted a petition signed by several other men supporting that claim. The colony then paid John thirty pounds for the money owed him.

In 1782, he and his sons David and Rufus signed a petition requesting a bridge be built over the Hoosick River. That request was not approved by the Vermont colony. The town of Hoosick was just across the river from Pownal and had a population of Puritans from New York. One can imagine that the Puritans wanted little to do with the rowdy Baptists, and a bridge would only complicate that situation. Thus, the Puritans rejected the "Bridge to Nowhere," as Pownal was certainly not a destination in their point of view, hence the title of this chapter.

John had the following children we documented from his final will written in 1805, read in court in December 1812. He left each of his children $1. A grandson, Salrava, was left $108.

- David, 1757–1826, Revolutionary War Patriot (drummer)
- Elijah, 1758–1796
- Poly Wilson, 1760–1812
- Rufus, 1761–1833, Revolutionary War Patriot
- Dr. John, 1767–1820, Revolutionary War Patriot
- Sylvester, 1768–1820
- Sally Clark, 1788–Unknown death date

Several researchers attribute the parentage of these children to David Perrigo Jr. and Abigail Brock, whose story is discussed earlier in the book. That seems to be an incorrect assignment, as four sons and two daughters are named in the will of John. Son Elijah was dead by 1796 and was not named in the will. Additionally, son Rufus claimed in his Revolutionary War pension application that he was born in New York. John had apparently lived there following his service in the French and Indian War. I do not believe that this David Perrigo Jr. ever lived in New York. Although not poof of relationship, the DAR recognizes—and has awarded memberships based on—both John's and his son's Revolutionary War service.

I sometimes wish to have been able to sit around the dinner table with this family and listen to the rich stories that might have been told. Think of it! Father served in both the French and Indian War and the Revolutionary War and was a very early settler in Vermont. Three sons served in the Revolutionary War. One son was a doctor and a surgeon in the war, and one was a storied legend of that war. A third son was also a noted fighter and changed units to stay in the fight. I cover their stories later in the book. This was a family of Patriots, and they would fight. I can also imagine that cousin Justus J. lived near and was about ten to twelve years of age during the latter stages of the war and that he wanted badly to make his mark in the world. It is clear that he did just that, but in a later war.

We are uncertain of John's burial location, but it was likely in Chittenden. We will tell the stories of his Patriot sons later in the book. His probate case is interesting for the fact that, after an inventory of his belongings and a listing of his assets, it was determined his estate was insolvent and that he owed more than could be paid to creditors.

As discussed in Chapter One, my search for the father of Justus Perrigo Sr. led me and other researchers to Pownal, Vermont. Neither Robert Bishop nor the Cutter Account produced the needed information; thus, a family mystery loomed for many years. My research led me and almost no one else to the belief that the father of Justus Sr. was David Perrigo, but proof remained elusive. First, there were too many Davids, and second, record-keeping in Pownal was lacking during the pre-revolution era. Remember, the record-keeping churches did not exist there at that time, and two colonies claimed Vermont but did little to keep vital records. It seemed clear that the father of Justus Sr. was likely a fourth-generation

Perrigo and that I would find him in Pownal, the believed birthplace of Justus. Three Perrigos of the third and fourth generations fit that proposal. Brothers John and David, and their father James Sr., and all lived in Pownal at the time of the birth of Justus. I found no other Perrigos in that area before the revolution. At that point it seemed possible to fit Justus in one of the two family groups because of the age of possible siblings, children of John or David. That effort produced an important conclusion. Justus was not a child of John, or James Sr. This conclusion can be drawn from the birth dates of their documented children—Justus does not fit there. He did, however, fit nicely into the family group of David and Susanna Varrel. Not proof of relationship, but perhaps preponderance of evidence? Let us see. David number three follows:

David Perrigo
Born: 1738
Died: After 1804
Birthplace: Unknown location in Massachusetts, maybe Bridgewater
Married: Susanna Varrel on 21 February 1765 in Gloucester, Essex, Massachusetts
Buried: Unknown location, but probably in Essex County, New York
Service: French and Indian War in Connecticut. Revolutionary War in the Continental Army in the Twenty-Sixth Regiment of Massachusetts. Later designated the Second Massachusetts Regiment. His father also served in that regiment during the revolution.
Lineage: Son Justus J. Sr., his son Justus Jr., his son Martin Vanburen, his son Andrew Jackson, and his daughter Blanche Francis Adams, my grandmother. He is almost certainly my fifth great-grandfather.
DAR: None
SAR: None

David is the unproven son of James Perrigo Sr. and Lydia Hayward of Stoughton, Massachusetts, and later Pownal, Vermont. I have not found church or city birth records recording that birth. Remember, I earlier discussed his father's family relocation from Stoughton in Norfolk County to Bridgewater, Plymouth County, around the year of his birth. They were quickly warned out of Bridgewater, and his birth may have simply not been recorded.

David married Susanna Varrel in Gloucester, Essex, Massachusetts, and I have those records. The distance from Plymouth to Gloucester is about sixty miles, and he was about twenty-seven years old. The marriage was in February 1765, and it seems he wasted no time in getting to Pownal, as we see him there with his father later that year, based on a census report from 1771. That report placed them in Pownal as early as 1765. Perhaps he arrived earlier, and he returned to marry, but that is speculation. Interestingly, that 1771 Vermont census report reflects him as being from Connecticut. Maybe he remained in Connecticut following the French and Indian War and remained there until his marriage.

His presence in Pownal is documented with several documents, petitions, and appointment notices.

He served in the French and Indian War for at least fifteen days in 1757, in the Connecticut Fourth Regiment Militia under the command of Colonel Wooster in the First Company. His brother Robert also served in the same unit in 1759. His cousin John Kemp Perrigo was killed while serving in the same unit in 1757. David would have been nineteen or twenty years old while serving. The book *Rolls of Connecticut Men in the French and Indian War 1755–1762* shown in the Reference Section establishes this fact, but it does not relate where they enlisted or served. His cousin John Kemp died in a hospital in Albany, New York, because of his injuries from an accidental shooting, so the unit may have been operating near Albany in 1757. His brother Robert also spent some time in that hospital the same year based on the above reference. I have researched French and Indian War records for several years and have observed that enlistments were for specific campaigns, not for a specific period as with the Revolutionary War and later conflicts. I believe that few men served in this war for only fifteen days. The records I found claimed fifteen days for David, but what I have is not an original record but an extract of an official record taken by a researcher a hundred years after the fact. That may only be part of the story. Remember I discussed earlier that brothers James Jr. and John also served in the French and Indian War but in a Massachusetts regiment at about the same time, and they also served in New York. Brother Robert went to Rhode Island after the war, James Jr. remained in Massachusetts, and John and David may have worked in New York or Connecticut and later relocated to Pownal with their father by 1765.

In 1787, David was appointed as surveyor and viewer of fences for Bennington County. The surveyor description is clear, but the viewer of fences should be explained. The Pownal area in Bennington County was being developed from the arrival of the first settlers twenty years earlier. David was among that early group. Descriptions of the land earlier in the book revealed that it was decent farming land as opposed to most Vermont land west of the mountains. Fencing was made mainly from stones cleared from the fields rather than wood rails. Once a fence was in place, it was difficult to adjust its location. Real property descriptions used landmarks such as rivers and large trees. Rivers changed over time and trees died. A fence, once in place, would become a long-term property boundary; therefore, locations of those fences were important. David would first need to know the basics of survey techniques and, second, need to be familiar with the community. This was an important job. It also indicates he was literate and a respected member of the community.

I found a petition signed by David in 1779 requesting that the Vermont legislature award him a land grant on the Missisquoi River. I found no evidence that the grant was awarded, so this might explain his next act.

David joined the Continental Army in Williamstown, Massachusetts, in 1780 and marched on 29 June that year. He served five and a half months and was discharged on 6 December that year. It is an interesting part of the story that his father, James Sr., joined the same unit in April 1777 and was AWOL by May that year, later returning for duty in January 1778 at Valley Forge. This is an interesting story that leads a person to imagine the many questions that are not easy to solve. David's service is recorded in *Massachusetts Soldiers and Sailors of the Revolutionary War*, Volume 12, page 187, as is his father's service. Neither of these men lived to claim a pension. James Sr. may not have been eligible because of his absence.

When this story is viewed in a larger perspective, there were eighteen Perrigo men, descendants of James Sr., living in and around Pownal at the time of the Revolutionary War. Ten of them were serving in the army at about the same time, starting in 1776 to 1780. The remaining eight men were too young to serve. Would this fact explain the actions of James Sr.? Did he return to care for the remaining families? When the regiment was converted to a Continental Line unit, an act that ensured the unit was leaving the colony, James Sr. opted to stay with the family. The count of serving Patriots was taken from the Figure 2 diagram.

I did not find any evidence of a land grant for his service in the Revolutionary War. I am not sure the colony of Massachusetts awarded any land grants, as the colony had no land to award, as did New York and Virginia.

We know of three children of David and Susanna:

- Frederick Howard, 1765–1850. Patriot of the Revolutionary War.
- Justus J. Sr., 1768–1832. War of 1812 and my fourth great-grandfather.
- Charles, 1770–1856

I have researched Wales Perrigo, who I believe may be a son of David and Susanna, but I have insufficient documentation to pursue this relationship further. Wales was born in 1774, making him a younger brother of Frederick, Justus, and Charles. I have further evidence of his children, but the lack of birth and other records in Pownal prevent listing him as a son of David; therefore, I have not shown him on the Figure 3 diagram. Wales lived in Duchess County, New York, and had several children, one of which was Wales Jr., a noted soldier of the Black Hawk War.

I am not sure of the death date of his wife Susanna Varrel, and I believe she may have died prior to the 1800 census, as it appears David may have lived with his son Frederick Howard at the time of that census. He was the only elderly person in that household with Frederick.

This David was the second David Perrigo of the fourth-generation Perrigo family. Remember, there was a third-generation David Perrigo. The other fourth-generation was David Jr., discussed above and outlined in the Perrigo Papers and the Cutter Account. That David married Abigail Brock and died in 1780 in New York. There were four other David Perrigos, all fifth-generation family members, and they will be discussed later in the book. I think I have established that there were multiple David Perrigos of Massachusetts and Vermont, and they were likely kin. I believe that David of Pownal was the son of James Perrigo Sr. and a brother of Robert, James Jr., and John. I believe the children I have attributed to these five men are correct, except for the fact that I have not adequately researched the female siblings. I believe it is reasonable to believe that this David Perrigo is the father of Justus Sr. and is my fifth great-grandfather. Thusly, I have placed him in the family tree in Figure 3 above.

I believe that David moved to New York before the 1790 census. His oldest son Frederick moved before this census, and David may have lived with or near him. I see David in the Willsborough, Essex County, tax rolls there in 1803 and 1804. I believe that he lived with his son Frederick Howard in the same location for the 1800 census, as there is one adult over forty-five along with his wife and family. His son Justus Sr. also lived near there. I have established his death date as after 1804 in Willsborough, New York, based on the tax list for that year. I have no other evidence of his death date.

I point out that another David Perrigo (1761–1826), the drummer and son of John, lived in and around Highgate, Vermont, after 1800, and that some researchers confuse these two Revolutionary War Patriots. I will discuss this David in the next chapter, as he is a fifth-generation Perrigo.

Chapter Six

"Gather the Drummer, the Fifer, and Doctors and Let's Go Fight"

The Fifth Generation

The first eleven Perrigos presented with the fifth-generation family are the children of Joseph Perrigo (1745–1840) and Annie Platt of Sussex County, New Jersey. They were discussed in the previous chapter with the Joseph Perrigo story. The documentation of their relationship to this family line consists of a family bible list (copied) belonging to son Abel Perrigo, as well as the Sussex First Baptist Church records extract discussed earlier and listed in the Reference Section of this book. I also found death records and marriage records that link several of them to Joseph and Annie. There were three children that were not listed in Abel's family bible but added later by family members. I will identify those members when I discuss them below. This recap of the earlier list summarizes the proposed siblings that will be further discussed in depth:

- David, 1771–1850. Not listed in the family bible but remained in Sussex County.
- Abel, 1773–1842. He remained in Sussex County and is listed in his family bible.
- Joseph M., 1774–1864. Married in Sussex County, served in the War of 1812, and remained in New York City for the remainder of his life. Listed in the family bible.
- James, 1776–1850. Moved to Guernsey, Ohio, and remained there. Listed in the family bible.
- Isaac, 1782–1864. Married in New Jersey but died in New York City. Listed in the family bible.
- William, 1784–Unknown death date. Little is known of him, and he is not listed in the family bible.
- Samuel, 1787–1830. Remained in Sussex County. Listed in the family bible.
- Margaret Young, 1791–1843. Remained in Sussex County after marriage and is listed in the family bible.
- Elizabeth Stratton, 1792–1851. Married in Sussex County in 1807 and moved via Pennsylvania to Ohio by 1817. Listed in the family bible.
- Annie, 1794–Unknown death date. She is not listed in the family bible.
- Eleazer, 1799–1878. Moved to Wayne County, Ohio, and is listed in the family bible.

David J. Perrigo

Born: About 1771

Died: After 1855

Birthplace: Probably Monmouth County, New Jersey

Married: Unknown

Buried: Unknown location

Service: Revolutionary War, Fourth Regiment of the New Jersey Militia

DAR: None

SAR: None

David is the proposed son of Thomas Perrigo and Anne Platt of Sussex County, New Jersey, and is a fifth-generation family member. He is the fourth David to be discussed in this book and is not discussed in either the Cutter Account or the Perrigo Papers.

I found David in a New Jersey state census of 1855 and in the 1850 federal census in Sussex County. The federal census shows him at an age consistent with a birth year of 1771, hence that is his assigned birth year shown above. This birth year is the year following the marriage of his mother and father. He was not listed in his brother Abel's family bible, but later family members had apparently added his name.

He served in the New Jersey Fourth Regiment during the Revolutionary War—with his service beginning on 10 March 1778—for nine months and was discharged in September 1779. He certainly did not serve at the age of nine, so was there a second David Perrigo of Sussex County, New Jersey?

I found no records of a marriage, but the 1830 federal census shows him in Sussex County with a man and woman of the appropriate ages with one other female family member, so he was possibly married.

The documentation I found that places him in Sussex County includes:

- Sussex County Tax List for June 1793
- The federal 1830 census for Sussex County
- The federal 1840 census for Sussex County
- The federal 1850 census for Sussex County
- The New Jersey 1855 census for Sussex County
- National Archives Revolutionary War roles

The date or location of his death is not known. The state 1855 census is the latest public record I found for him.

Abel Perrigo

Born: 3 February 1773

Died: 3 November 1842

Birthplace: Monmouth County, New Jersey

Married: Mary Little on 4 March 1799 in Sussex County, New Jersey

Buried: Unknown location

Abel is a fifth-generation Perrigo family member and the son of Joseph Perrigo and Annie Platt of Sussex County, New Jersey. He is listed in the records of First Baptist Church of Wantage, Sussex County, as a son of Joseph. His family bible also reflects that he is the son of Joseph.

He married Mary Little on 4 March 1799 in Sussex County. He and Mary had eight children. I have those marriage records. The children were:

- John, 1801–1874. Married Clarissa (Clara) Jane Conklin and died in Poweshiek County, Iowa.
- Moses C., 1803–1868. Married Sarah Ross and remained in Sussex County.
- Adelide Townsend, 1807–1827. Married Zebulan Townsend and remained in Sussex County.
- Samuel, 1807–1872. Married Rosetta (last name unknown) and remained in Sussex County as a farmer and landowner.
- Mahala Havens, 1810–Unknown death date.
- Jobe Little, 1811–1887. Married Cynthia A. Cunningham. They had one child and settled in Lafayette, Allen, Indiana.
- Catherine Ann Stinson, 1814–Unknown death date.
- William M., 1816–1864. Married Mary Ann Riggs and moved to Bowman's Creek, Wyoming County, Pennsylvania. He died as a Civil War POW at Andersonville, Georgia. He was a soldier in G Company of the Pennsylvania 143rd Infantry Regiment.

Abel spent his entire life in and around Sussex County, New Jersey. I believe I will eventually locate his burial location.

Joseph M. Perrigo

Born: 1774

Died: 17 April 1864

Birthplace: Sussex County, New Jersey

Married: Margaret Wiggins on 23 October 1798 in Wantage, Sussex County, New Jersey

Buried: Unknown location in New York City

Joseph M. is a fifth-generation Perrigo and the son of Joseph Perrigo and Annie Platt. His birth is shown in the Wantage First Baptist Church records, and he is recorded in his brother Abel's family bible. He married Margaret Wiggins in Wantage, New Jersey, in 1798 and soon moved to New York City. They were married in the Dutch Reformed Church of Clove Valley, Wantage, Sussex County, New Jersey. I have those records.

He served in the War of 1812 in the New York Militia Second Regiment commanded by Colonel Wood during the last three months of 1814. Ninety days was the normal militia enlistment period for that war. Forty years later in 1854, he made a claim pertaining to his service in 1814. He claimed that he had received a forty-acre land grant for that service but had never been paid for his service or for the equipment and clothing he had been required to furnish for his own use. He valued that equipment at $87. He was reimbursed $50 for the equipment but probably not for his pay, as his pay records show clearly that he was paid about $8 per month for three months.

Joseph lived his entire adult life in New York City as a cart driver according to census records. He and Margret may have had three children, but I was unable to confirm their names. I have a copy of his will, but I was unable to read the names. I also have the newspaper article listing his death date and location.

James Perrigo (Perego)

Born: 22 September 1776
Died: 10 September 1850
Birthplace: New Jersey
Married: Mary Jane Miller in 1800 in Belmont, Ohio
Buried: Unknown location in Guernsey, Ohio

James is the fifth-generation son of Joseph Perrigo and Annie Platt of Sussex County, New Jersey. He is listed in his brother Abel's family bible and the Sussex County Baptist Church records. He later listed Ohio as his birthplace in the 1850/1860 census records, but he seems to have been born in New Jersey.

He married Mary Jane Miller in Belmont, Ohio, and they farmed near Millwood, Guernsey, Ohio, for the remainder of their lives. They had five children:

- Isaac, 1801–1871. He married Sarah Hartley, and they had six children and remained in Millwood, Guernsey, Ohio.
- Margret Grier, 1805–1855. She married Henry Grier Jr., and they had nine children and settled in Rendville, Perry County, Ohio.
- Nancy Ward, 1807–1876. She married David Ward, and they lived in Jefferson, Noble, Ohio.
- Sarah Galloway, 1811–1891. She married Enoch Galloway, and they remained in Guernsey, Ohio.
- John, 1815–1885. John was born in Belmont, Ohio, and married Matilda Samantha Clary in 1838 in Guernsey, Ohio. By 1870 he was living in Monroe, Green County, Wisconsin, and later moved with a son to Oregon County, Missouri. He died and is buried there. Name often spelled as Perego.

I will make an exception of not publishing a sixth-generation Perrigo line in this instance because of my discovery of a second Missouri Perrigo line previously unknown by myself. The spelling variations of their name has changed to an extent I cannot attribute to spelling errors on one or two documents. Spelling variations included Perigoy and Prego. I found death certificates and tombstones with Perego, and I think this was the most-often-used variation. For an unknown reason, they changed the spelling of their name. They are clearly linked to the New Jersey Perrigo line.

The **sixth-generation** children of John and Matilda mentioned above were:

- Maria Jane Lanning, 1840–1915. Married Jerimiah "Jerry" Lanning. They had nine children and remained in Guernsey County, Ohio.
- Sarah/Sadie DePriest, 1844–1921. Married Christopher "Kit" DePriest, and she died in Oregon County, Missouri.
- Permila Wilson Bourner, 1847–1934. She married (1) William Wilson and (2) Caleb Bourner and died in Newark, Licking, Ohio.
- James (Perego), 1849–1939. Became a postmaster in Shepherdstown, Belmont, Ohio, and died in Oregon, Missouri.
- William Henry (Perego), 1852–1942. Married Helen Minich, and they had nine children. They moved to Oregon County, Missouri, before 1900 and farmed there.
- Samuel Greenbury (Perego), 1855–1899. Married Martha Jane Williams, and they moved to Oregon County, Missouri. They had seven children.
- Isaac 1856– Unknown death date.
- Amanda Harrington, 1860–1939. She married Oliver James Harrington, and they lived in Oregon County, Missouri.
- Florence, 1861–Unknown death date. Little is known of her except she is listed in her father's 1870 census.
- Joseph, 1864–Unknown death date. Little is known of him except he is listed in his father's 1870 census.

I will add that I found several photos of William Henry Perrigo (Perego) listed above, and he claimed to have not shaved since the age of twenty-one. He had the most distinguished, well-groomed white beard I have seen. He was nearly ninety and died the year of my birth. He would have been my fifth cousin four times removed.

Now, back to **the fifth-generation** lines:

Isaac Perrigo
Born: 1782
Died: 1864 New York, New York
Birthplace: Sussex County, New Jersey
Married: Cynthia Howell on 7 January 1809 in Sussex County
Buried: Unknown location

Isaac in a fifth-generation Perrigo and the son of Joseph Perrigo and Annie Platt of Sussex County, New Jersey. His name is listed in his brother Abel's family bible, and he is also listed in the Sussex Baptist Church records. He married Cynthia Howell in Sussex County and moved to New York, New York. Little else is known of him.

William Perrigo
Born: 1784
Died: Unknown
Birthplace: Sussex County, New Jersey
Married: Unknown
Buried: Unknown

William was not listed in Abel's family bible.

Samuel Perrigo
Born: 1790
Died: Before 1850
Birthplace: Sussex County, New Jersey
Married: Mary Bohanon on 18 April 1813 in Sussex, New Jersey
Buried: Unknown

Samuel was the fifth-generation son of Joseph Perrigo and Annie Platt of Sussex County, New Jersey. He was listed in his brother Abel's family bible, but I found few records of him. He married Mary Bohanon in Sussex County, and I have those records.

His wife, Mary, was living with her daughter Sarah in Sandstone, Jackson, Michigan, at the time of the federal 1850 census, but Samuel was not part of the family.

Margaret Perrigo Young

Born: 1791

Died: 1843

Birthplace: Sussex County, New Jersey

Married: John Young on 4 October 1807 in Sussex County, New Jersey

Buried: Unknown location in Sussex County, New Jersey

Margaret is a fifth-generation Perrigo and daughter of Joseph Perrigo and Annie Platt. She was listed in Abel's family bible, but I found no additional documentation for her.

Elizabeth Perrigo Stratton

Born: 31 March 1792

Died: 9 August 1861

Birthplace: Sussex County, New Jersey

Married: Joseph Stratton on 5 December 1807 in Sussex County, New Jersey

Buried: Canaan Center Cemetery in Canaan, Wayne County, Ohio

Elizabeth was the daughter of Joseph Perrigo and Annie Platt of Sussex County, New Jersey. She is listed in her brother Abel's family bible and in the Sussex Baptist Church records. She married Joseph B. Stratton in Sussex County on 5 December 1807. I have those marriage records.

Joseph was the son of Revolutionary War Patriot Daniel Stratton and Shady Grub also of Sussex County. Joseph and Elizabeth both belonged to the Quaker Church in New Jersey. After the birth of their first four children, the Strattons began their migration to Ohio through Pennsylvania. Their son Daniel was born in Pennsylvania in 1817.

After arriving in Canaan Township in Wayne County, Ohio, they purchased a 160-acre farm in 1817. This was frontier territory, and they encountered Indian problems for several years after arriving. Joseph was well educated and served as a schoolteacher for several years while doing carpenter work and farming. He was elected as justice of the peace for the township several times during his life, as well as to other county offices. They were members of the Baptist Church in Ohio. Elizbeth's brother Eleazer Perrigo also lived in Canaan Township.

I discovered several stories about this well-respected family. One involved an incident in which they came upon an Indian youth who was very ill and near death. They took the child in and nursed him back to health and returned him to his tribe. Within a year, the Strattons were experiencing a very bad winter with little food when they discovered someone had left a full dear carcass hanging on their front porch. They had experienced a payback for a good deed. Another story was told in which Elizabeth had let her fire go cold and therefore took a kettle on horseback to a neighbor to obtain a few live coals. She took the coals in the kettle and started home as quickly as possible and grabbed an apple switch to prod the horse along. After arriving home, she threw the switch to the ground. She later discovered the switch had taken root, as a pear tree stood in the middle of where she had planted a garden. That story is told in a published book now in the Wayne County Historical Society.

The Strattons remained in Wayne County and had thirteen children. These children are documented with several resources: the 1850 federal census and Wayne County published history stories with family names. Their children were:

- Anna Miller, 1809–1852. Married Joseph M. Miller, and they had eight children and lived in Mount Cory, Hancock County, Ohio.
- William, 1810–1857. Married Elizabeth Denning and lived in Mount Cory, Hancock County, Ohio.
- Mark, 1812–1889. Married Mary Shellenbarger, and they lived in Largo, Wabash County, Indiana.
- Thomas, 1815–1864. Married Celia Wade Jones, and they lived in Union, Hassan, Hancock County, Ohio.
- Francis, 1817–1844. She died in Wayne County at the age of twenty-seven.
- Daniel, 1817–1890. He married Christena Meyers, and they remained in Wayne County.
- Sarah Parmenter, 1821–1895. She married Alfred Parmenter, and they remained in Canaan, Wayne County.
- Cyrus, 1823–1896. He married Sarah Meyers, and they remained in Canaan, Wayne County.
- Margaret Myers, 1825–1873. She married John William Myers, and they remained in Wayne County.
- Elizabeth Rumbaugh, 1829–1898. She married William M. Rumbaugh, and they moved to Linn, Oregon.
- Catherine Heckert, 1830–1873. She married Jonas Heckert, and they remained in Wayne County.
- Mary Sanders, 1832–1879. She married Isaac D. Sanders, and they remained in Canaan, Wayne County.
- Jane, 1835–1841. She died at the age of six.

Annie Perrigo Young

Born: 1794

Died: Unknown death date

Birthplace: Sussex County, New Jersey

Married: Peter Young

Buried: Unknown location

Annie was not listed in Abel Perrigo's family bible, but her name was added by family later based on census information. I found no further information on her.

Eleazer Perrigo

Born: 1799

Died: 1878

Birthplace: Sussex County, New Jersey

Married: Amy Stratton in 1830

Buried: Unknown location in Mount Cory, Hancock County, Ohio

Eleazer is a fifth-generation Perrigo and son of Joseph Perrigo and Annie Platt of Sussex County, New Jersey. He was listed in his brother Abel's family bible and in the Wantage, Sussex Baptist Church records.

He had moved to Wayne County, Ohio, by the time he married Amy Stratton there. He was a farmer and owned his land near Canaan, Wayne County, Ohio. Eleazer's wife, Amy Stratton, was the daughter of Daniel Stratton, who was a brother of Joseph Stratton, the husband of Eleazer's sister, Elizabeth Perrigo Stratton discussed earlier. Eleazer and Amy had seven children. They were:

- Mary Cook, 1829–1901. She married Live Cook, and they had six children and lived in Union City, Hancock, Ohio.
- Joseph, 1831–1911. He married Nancy Clymer in 1850 and moved to Linn County, Iowa, by 1853. He served in the Union Army during the Civil War and was wounded. He reenlisted as a blacksmith. Later, he was a mason in Cedar Rapids, Iowa. He had ten children.
- Sarah Handshy, 1836–1928. She married John Handshy, and they had four children and moved to West Mineral, Cherokee County, Kansas, where he was a miller.
- Lucinda Meeds, 1839–1898. She married John H. Meeds, and they had three children. They remained in Union City, Hancock County, Ohio.
- Catherine, 1843–Unknown death date.
- Lavina Wilkins, 1843–1925. She married Absalom Wilkins. They had six children and remained in Union, Hancock County, Ohio.

Now we return to the Massachusetts **fifth-generation** Perrigo line:

Ezekiel Perrigo

Born: 10 December 1758

Died: 5 January 1803 in Sprague, Connecticut

Birthplace: Gloucester, Essex, Massachusetts

Married: 28 October 1772 to Alice Webb in New London, Connecticut

Buried: Unknown location

Service: None

Ezekiel Perrigo was a fifth-generation Perrigo and the son of David Perrigo Jr. and Abigail Brock of Gloucester, Massachusetts. We know he is the son of David Jr. and Abigail as I have the birth records consisting of the town records. Other researchers have named his father as John Kemp Perrigo, but John probably never married, having died in the French and Indian War at the age of twenty-two.

Ezekiel married Alice Webb in New London, Connecticut, on 28 October 1772, and I have those records. He remained in the New London area for the remainder of his life and had at least twelve children. Their church records record their marriage, the births of their children, and his death on 5 January 1803 in Sprague, Connecticut.

His wife, Alice, was a sixth-generation descendant of Governor William Bradford. He was a 1620 *Mayflower* pilgrim arriving from Holland after leaving England and was one of the first governors of the Plymouth Colony. The Bradford house remains standing in Connecticut as a historic landmark. The Bradford plantation home also still stands, and I have included a picture of that home in Figure 12 in Chapter Seven below. The Bradfords left Plymouth and settled in Rhode Island, hence the Rhode Island home. His life story is very interesting and is outlined in the book *Descendants of Governor William Bradford* shown in the reference section below. This is a well-researched family line, and I will not list the proofs of relationships, but I did find birth records for Alice. Ezekiel's marriage seems to explain his moving to Connecticut from Massachusetts. This is the lineage of Alice back to her great-grandfather William Bradford III:

1. Parents of Alice:
   - Ebenezer Webb, 1718–1803. Revolutionary War Patriot of Windham, Massachusetts.
   - Ruth Waldo Crane, 1749–1796
2. Parents of Ebenezer:
   - Arthur Samuel Webb, 1697–1779. Lived in Windham, Connecticut, and died in Rockingham, Windham, Vermont.
   - Hannah Bradford Ripley, 1685–1751
3. Parents of Hannah Bradford Ripley:
   - Joshua Ripley Sr., 1658–1739. Born in Plymouth, Massachusetts. Died in Windham, Connecticut.

- Dr. Hannah Bradford Ripley, 1662–1738. The only medical doctor in Windham for several years.
4. Parents of Dr. Hannah Bradford Ripley:
   - William Bradford IV, 1624–1703. Second governor of Plymouth. Born and died in Plymouth, Massachusetts. Major in King Philip's War.
   - Alice Richards, 1627–1671
5. Parents of William Bradford IV:
   - William Bradford III, 1588–1657. First governor of the Plymouth Colony and a Mayflower Compact signer.
   - Alice Carpenter, 1590–1670

I will note that Ezekiel's marriage to Alice Webb is interesting in that this is the second marriage of a Perrigo to a *Mayflower* Descendant, with James Perrigo's marriage to Lydia Hayward being the first. Her ancestor John Alden was a next-door neighbor of William Bradford in the original Plymouth village before the Bradfords' move to Rhode Island.

I found no records indicating Ezekiel ever served in the military. He probably did not travel far in his life as it is only about 120 miles from his birth town of Gloucester to Norwich.

Their children were:

- Betsey, 1773–1851. May have never married.
- Rodentha, 1774–1850. May have never married.
- Poly Griswold, 1776–1828. Married Sylvester Griswold and lived in Vermont.
- Eleanor, 1778–Unknown death date.
- Azel, 1780–Unknown death date.
- Boltum, 1782–Unknown death date.
- Susanna Tubbs, 1784–1859. Married Samuel Tubbs and lived in New London, Connecticut.
- Olive Crocker, 1786–1859. Married Warren Crocker and lived in Massachusetts.
- Samuel, 1789–1856. Married Isabel Nichols and lived in Windham, Connecticut.
- Abigail, 1791–1819. Died in Lisbon, Rhode Island, at the age of twenty-seven.
- Roswell, 1793–Unknown death date.
- Ruby, 1796–1800. Died as a youth.

We found the birth dates and the names of their children in the Governor William Bradford records and in the Lisbon church records.

As I researched this family group, I was struck by the fact that Ezekiel and Alice Webb had twelve children, eleven of which were daughters. Only three of them married. The son Samuel married, but I believe he never had children. That Perrigo line quickly ended with no one to carry on the name. Three of their daughters had children, so descendants of those women are likely eligible to claim Mayflower Descendant status.

David Perrigo III

Born: 7 September 1760

Died: Possibly by 1800

Birthplace: Gloucester, Essex, Massachusetts

Married: Nancy Sherman on 28 September 1801 in Hancock, Massachusetts

Buried: Unknown location

Service: None

David is a fifth-generation Perrigo. Gloucester church records establish he was the son of David Perrigo Jr. and Abigail Brock. He is the fifth David presented thus far in this project, and I have found few records documenting his life after his birth in Massachusetts. I found him in the 1790 Massachusetts census at an appropriate age. His father, David, was dead by 1780, so this was likely the only David Perrigo living in Massachusetts in 1790. I have found a marriage record in Massachusetts attesting to a marriage to Nancy Sherman on 28 September 1801, making him forty-one years of age at that time. I found little else concerning him. It would be easy to confuse this David with the drummer of Pownal who was born in 1761, and David, the son of Joseph discussed above. They were nearly the same age, but clearly different men.

I do not believe that David III had children.

John Perrigo

Born: 12 August 1764 (Baptism)

Died: Before 1790

Birthplace: Gloucester, Essex, Massachusetts

Married: Unknown

Buried: Unknown location

Service: None known

John is the fifth-generation son of David Perrigo Jr. and Abigail Brock and was born in Gloucester, Essex, Massachusetts. This is a proven relationship, with his church birth records reflecting his father and mother. I have found no marriage records, nor does he appear on the 1790 census, so it is suspected he died before that date. I should note that my census record search for him extended to all the New England states.

Joseph Hewes Perrigo

Born: 7 October 1763

Died: 29 August 1843 in Grandby, Oswego, New York

Birthplace: Providence, Rhode Island

Married: 17 November 1794 in Plainfield, Windham, Connecticut to Meriam Maxwell

Buried: Unknown location

Service: Rhode Island Line in the Continental Army from 6 March 1781 to 25 December 1783

DAR: None

SAR: None

Joseph is a fifth-generation Perrigo and the son of Robert Perrigo and Sarah Shorey of Providence, Rhode Island. He is the fifth Joseph we have featured in this book. He was born in Providence, Rhode Island, and resided there until he was eighteen years old and joined the Rhode Island Regiment commanded by Colonel Olney on 2 March 1781 for the duration of the war. He joined in Providence, Exeter County. His company commander was Captain William Allen. We know he is the son of Robert and Sarah Perrigo because of sworn statements made by him pertaining to his military pension in 1824, and this location is consistent with the location of his parents at the time of his birth. Remember, his father also served in the Revolutionary War in a local militia, as did his brother Dr. Robert.

He served as a regimental fifer during his service in this Continental Line army unit. This fact makes him part of the musical allusion in the chapter title. After enlistment, he soon marched to Virginia and later participated in the Siege of Yorktown, the final campaign of the war. After the end of the war, his unit moved to Oswego, New York, where he stated he was injured by frostbite to his hands and legs. He was discharged on 25 December 1783 at Saratoga, New York. The *Regimental Book* shown in the reference section below gives his occupation at the time of enlistment as laborer and describes that he had dark hair and stood five feet, seven inches tall. This book gives his enlistment date as 5 April 1781, and other records, including statements made by him in sworn affidavits, show either 2 or 6 March of that year.

Following the war, he returned to Exeter County, Rhode Island, and was married about one year later to Meriam Maxwell of Plainfield, Windham County, Connecticut. They were married by a justice of the peace in Plainfield and lived with her family for about one year after their marriage. They then moved to Salem, New York, where he was able to borrow the money to buy a farm. He farmed the remainder of his life until he could no longer work. One can speculate that he became familiar with New York while serving in the military and chose to return there to farm.

His father, Robert, had also moved to Washington County and died there in 1808. He and Meriam had one son. His son confirmed this fact in a sworn statement in his 1832 pension request. Rhode Island has five counties now, but apparently there were three counties at that time. Their son was:

- Robert, 1785–1865. Remained in New York and had nine children.

He filed for a pension in Washington County, New York, claiming he was sixty-seven years of age and that neither he nor his wife were able to work and that they had no sources of income. It appears that his initial pension request was not approved because of lack of documentation of some sort. He reapplied in 1824 in Washington County, and his request was held until he could explain why he had waited so long to make the claim. The pension act was passed in 1818, and he would have been eligible after that date. While there was no disability requirement to make a pension claim, it was common practice for the claimant to make a needs statement. One can only guess why he waited. He was not married when he served, so his wife Meriam would not have been eligible for a pension on his behalf until the 1833 Pension Act. She did make such a claim in 1834, and it was approved. It appears he lived with his only son later in his life. He died on 29 August 1843 in Granby, Oswego County, New York.

Dr. Robert Perrigo Jr.

Born: 4 November 1765
Died: 13 August 1829 in Erie County, Pennsylvania
Birthplace: Providence County, Rhode Island
Married: Anna Nancy Rock
Buried: Old Bristol Farm Cemetery, Girard, Erie County, Pennsylvania
Service: Rhode Island Militia during the Revolutionary War and the New York Militia during the War of 1812
DAR: None
SAR: None

Dr. Robert Jr. is the fifth-generation son of Robert Perrigo and Sarah Shorey of Providence, Rhode Island. He was born in Providence County, Rhode Island, and at the age of sixteen joined the Rhode Island Regiment for the Revolutionary War in 1782. His length of enlistment was nine months, and he was discharged on 20 December 1782. Unlike his older brother Joseph Hewes, who joined the Continental Army, Robert joined the militia. It is likely the Continental Army could not enlist a sixteen-year-old man, but the militia was more than willing to accommodate him. MacGunnigle's *Regimental Book* reflects he was a laborer and that he was five feet, four and a half inches tall and had brown hair.

I did not find proof of his birth to father Robert (born 1729), but I found the pension application of his brother Joseph Hewes. In this application, Joseph Hewes mentioned a business dealing with his brother Robert, who was then deceased. This application was dated 1832, and Dr. Robert Jr. died in 1829. The Perrigo Papers are supportive of this relationship.

Robert married Anna Nancy Rock—daughter of John Rock and Anna Nancy of Argyle, New York—at an unknown date, but probably after having moved from Rhode Island, as did his father and brother. He and Anna Nancy had one son:

- Dr. James Rock Perrigo, 1795–1860. Married Drusilla Babcock and later moved to Layfette County, Wisconsin. Children settled in Illinois and Iowa. He is the third Perrigo doctor we have discussed in this book.

He served in the New York Militia as a lieutenant during the War of 1812 period and later moved to Erie County, Pennsylvania. At some point in his career, he became a doctor, and his headstone in Pennsylvania is so marked. He is buried in the Old Bristol Farm Cemetery in Girard, Pennsylvania. I will discuss what we know of his medical career later in this chapter.

I found claims presented by Dr. Robert Perrigo of Rhode Island for reimbursement for medical supplies that he had used while serving as a medical doctor during the Revolutionary War. That claim was approved and paid. Bob Bishop briefly mentions a Dr. Perrigo who served in that war, and I speculate he was referring to the son of Robert. I simply cannot attribute medical practice to Robert Jr., the son of Robert, during the revolution because of his age of sixteen and his military records, which I have. There was almost certainly another Dr. Robert Perrigo of Rhode Island who was a Patriot, and I doubt if he was related to this Perrigo line.

James Perrigo III
Born: 3 July 1774
Died: 6 June 1834 in Wrentham, Norfolk, Massachusetts
Birthplace: Wrentham, Norfolk, Massachusetts
Married: Comfort Chenery on 18 August 1794 in Wrentham
Buried: Wrentham
Service: None

James III is a fifth-generation Perrigo and the son of James Perrigo Jr. and Elizabeth Petee of Wrentham. He is listed in his father's will as well as Wrentham birth records. I use the suffix of III in this instance as he is the proven son of James Jr., and James Jr. is the son of James. As discussed above, he used James Jr. on the face of a clock he made, but it was common practice for subsequent sons to use Jr. as opposed to a numerical designation. He used Jr. on many of his legal documents. This clock is a very high-quality clock with a second hand, a complication that required skills not often encountered in the colonial period. As with his father's clocks, his clocks are highly prized antiques, and they display the best in colonial craftsmanship. I found a newspaper advertisement he published in which he mentions he had recently hired a master clockmaker and would also repair clocks. The clock mentioned is pictured here.

Carved Cherry Tall Case Clock, James Perrigo, Jr., Wrentham or Franklin, Massachusetts, early 19th century, the arched hood with freestanding columns enclosing a white-painted polychrome and gilt iron dial showing an exotic bird in the arch, with floral spandrels, seconds hand, and calendar aperture, lettered "J. Perrigo, Junr:," with brass weight-driven eight-day movement, the waist with thumbmolded door flanked by lambrequin corners, on ogee bracket feet, old surface, (imperfections), ht. 86 in.

FIGURE 10: James Perrigo III Clock

Image and information source: Skinner Auctions www.skinnerinc.com

James and Comfort had five children:

- David, 1794–1881. Remained in Wrentham his entire life.
- Charles, 1798–1806. Died as a youth.
- Clarinda Blake, 1800–1842. Remained in Norfolk County.
- Caroline, 1804–1871. Never married and died of typhoid.
- Hannah Alexander, 1808–1873. Married and lived in Suffolk County, Massachusetts.

He remained and worked in the Wrentham area his entire life. Their children are all proven by the excellent Wrentham birth and death records; however, I could find no will or probate records for him. I found craftsperson files documenting his clockmaker status, as well as a Masonic lodge membership card.

John Perrigo
Born: 21 August 1773
Died: 10 November 1829
Birthplace: Wrentham, Massachusetts
Married: Sally Adams Gould on 8 December 1799 in Wrentham, Massachusetts
Buried: Unknown location in Wrentham
Service: None

John is a fifth-generation Perrigo family member and the son of James Perrigo Jr. and Elizabeth Petee of Wrentham. He married Sally Adams Gould on 8 December 1799 in Wrentham. He is listed on his father's will and in several Wrentham birth, marriage, and death records. He and Sally had five children:

- Eliza Simmons, 1800–1884. Married a minister and had two children. One child became a college professor. She remained in Massachusetts her entire life.
- Roxa P. Fales, 1802–1894. Married Silas Fales, had five children, and remained in Massachusetts for her entire life.
- James Milton, 1805–1875. Married Sarah Bird had seven children, including one son, and remained in Massachusetts for his entire life. He was a farmer.
- Sarah Adams Daniels, 1809–1880. Married Lewis G. Daniels, had three sons, and remained in Massachusetts for the remainder of her life.
- Caleb S., 1811–1844. Married Mary H. Greenman in 1841 in Wrentham at age thirty and died in 1844 of consumption in Wrentham. His only son, James Greenman (1842–1873), became a railroad conductor and was killed in a train accident in 1873 in Rhode Island.

John died at the age of fifty-six in Wrentham, and his wife survived. It is speculated that he was a farmer, as I found that his oldest son, James Milton, died in Wrentham in 1875 and was a farmer.

Jared Perrigo

Born: 25 August 1775 and baptized 27 August 1775

Died: Unknown death date, but probably after 1805

Birthplace: Wrentham, Massachusetts

Married: Unknown

Buried: Unknown location

Service: None known

Jared is the son of James Perrigo Jr. and Elizabeth Petee of Wrentham. I have his Wrentham birth records, but little other evidence of his life. He was listed in his father's 1805 will, but no census records were found for him before or after the 1805 will.

Robert Perrigo

Born: 10 July 1779

Died: 15 July 1834 in Westmorland County, New Brunswick, Canada

Birthplace: Wrentham, Massachusetts

Married: Hannah Page on 12 January 1803 in Norfolk, Massachusetts

Buried: Moncton, Westmorland County, New Brunswick, Canada

Service: None

Robert is a fifth-generation Perrigo and the son of James Perrigo Jr. and Elizabeth Petee of Wrentham, Massachusetts. He is listed in his father's will and in Wrentham birth records. He married Hannah Page in Walpole, Norfolk, Massachusetts, on 12 January 1803. We have those marriage records. His first two children were born in Massachusetts, with the remaining children being born in either Maine or in New Brunswick, Canada, where he died and is buried. He was a farmer in Maine and later in Canada. He and Hannah had nine children:

- George E., 1804–1894. Married Elvira Rodgers, had seven children, and lived in Milo, Piscataquis, Maine. He was a farmer.
- Warren M., 1805–1851. Married Prudence M. Beckwith, had seven children, and lived in Westmorland, New Brunswick, Canada.
- Asa Page, 1807–1878. Married Lillian Crandall and lived in Salisbury, Westmorland, New Brunswick, Canada.
- Lucy Piper, 1808–1895. Married Ruben Piper and lived in Manitowoc Rapids, Wisconsin.
- Robert Leander, 1811–1867. Married Anne Crandall, had one son, and lived in Salisbury, Westmorland, New Brunswick, Canada.

- Hannah M. Wentworth, 1813–1888. Married Freedom Wentworth and later Ambrose Arnold and lived in Appleton, Knox, Maine.
- Artemas Clinton, 1813–1855. Married Elizabeth Ann Parlett and later Lovina Snider and lived in Donavan, Iroquois, Illinois.
- James Greenman, 1815–1867. Fought in the Massachusetts Union Army during the Civil War.
- Charles, 1818–1890. Married Susan F. Hodgdon, had six children, and lived in Piscataquis, Maine.

He moved at least once in Canada and is shown on the 1825 census in Montreal, Quebec, Canada, with his family.

Sergeant David Perrigo

Born: 1757

Died: 27 May 1826 at Highgate, Vermont

Birthplace: Keensboro, now Whitehall, New York

Married: (1) Susan Hayward and (2) Eunice Hurlburt

Buried: Unknown, but probably Georgia Township, Franklin County, Vermont

Service: Continental Army, "Green Mountain Boys"

Rank: Sergeant/Drummer

Service Dates: 26 December 1776 to December 1780

DAR: AO89011

SAR: None

David is a fifth-generation Perrigo and the son of John Perrigo and Mary (possibly Flint) of Vermont. While I could find no birth records, he stated in his 1814 pension hearing that he was fifty-seven years old. Statements made by his wife at later pension hearings following is death seem to support that date, so his birth year is attributed to those statements. He is listed in his father's 1810 will. While there is some confusion about his birthplace over the course of military enlistments and pension requests, he was certainly born close to Pownal, Vermont, or New York. That is where his father spent several years, and David is the proven son of John. He signed at least one petition in Pownal along with his father. That petition was the "Bridge to Nowhere" petition of 1780, which also contained the signature of his brother Rufus.

This David is the sixth David Perrigo I have presented in this book, and he is discussed by Bob Bishop in the Perrigo Papers as well as in the Cutter Account. Both those resources incorrectly attribute his birth to a different father. In fairness to Mr. Bishop, he asserts that this David was the son of a lady with the family name Flint, and that her husband and the father of David was Joseph Perrigo. I believe this statement was probably based on New York marriage documents claiming that Joseph Perrigo married a Flint. I have been unable to locate those documents; moreover, I have not documented a fourth-generation Joseph Perrigo except the Joseph of the New Jersey line. The fifth-generation Joseph Hewes Perrigo was clearly not the father of this David. I recommend that readers review the Figure 3 chart to visualize this issue. I maintain that the mother of David was probably Mary Flint based on the will of John, but that is speculation. I believe that the will of John Perrigo sets this issue to rest, and the petition signed by John and David and Rufus, seemingly of the same household, reinforces that position. I will risk further confusion by asserting that the Joseph Perrigo of New Jersey also had a son named David! He was also a Revolutionary War Patriot. They are certainly different David Perrigos. I discussed the New Jersey line at length earlier in the book.

David enlisted in Captain Simeon Smith's company of Seth Warner's regiment of the New York line on 26 December 1776 for three years as a sergeant and drummer. It should be noted that Vermont and Connecticut were not then colonies but were considered territories of New York. David was from Vermont and possibly a logger by trade (Perrigo Papers). He was discharged at Ft. George, New York, in December 1780 and applied for a pension on 24 April 1818, and it was approved. The pension certificate number was 12886, and his pension number was W19981. His pension was for $8 per month, and he was wounded several times in combat. His service as a regimental drummer probably led to one or more injuries, as they were good targets for the enemy. They were also not armed. Vermont records show that he enlisted in the Vermont Militia in December 1776 but only served for eight days, and that he was discharged when he joined the Continental Army on 26 December 1776.

David saw a lot of action and fought with some historical figures of the war. Colonel Seth Warner's regiment was known as the Green Mountain Boys. This unit was initially established by Ethan Allen prior to the revolution. It became well known for its role in and around Quebec and was well respected by General Washington. During the winter of 1775–1776, the regiment was involved in the siege of Quebec after Benedict Arnold was wounded in an attack by the British who were attempting to regain control of the Quebec fortress. The army at Quebec was hit by an epidemic of smallpox and lost many men. Colonel Warner was not a doctor, but he had a great deal of practical knowledge of remedies. He encouraged his men to inoculate themselves by making an incision and exposing themselves to the disease. This would give them a mild form of the disease which they could survive, but they would infect those around them that had not been inoculated. This practice was prohibited by George Washington, but it worked for them. In the spring, British warships came to Quebec, and Warner's regiment abandoned the fort. Colonel Warner served not only as commander of the retreat, but he served in the rear party and helped tend to the sick. They were being pursued by the British, and he saved their backside as they retreated. They lived to fight again.

On 5 July 1776, Congress authorized New York to raise a regiment consisting of the Green Mountain Boys. This act was "suggested" by General Washington. This was controversial in the colony, as the Green Mountain Boys had been engaged in some fighting against the colony when they attempted to redraw the line between the colony and the territory of Vermont. New York lost in that attempt, and the Green Mountain Boys were considered terrorists by the colony. The Green Mountain Boys were also singularly responsible for preventing the Vermont territory from seceding from the colonies and joining with Quebec prior to the revolution. David lived in Vermont at the time, but Congress could not authorize a territory to raise a unit, so New York was directed to authorize this regiment. Colonel Warner was again elected as commander of the reorganized unit by his men, probably because of his skill in taking care of them and because he was a pretty good leader. David Perrigo joined the unit in December of 1776. I have no way of determining if he previously fought with the original Green Mountain Boys prior to the war, as they did not keep good records, but it is certain that he would have been aware of their history and may have served with the regiment prior to his enlistment in the Continental Army.

In January 1777, the regiment was quartered on Mount Independence. That summer, they were involved in several battles at Ticonderoga, Hubbardston, and Bennington. Their losses were heavy, with both disease and combat injuries. In his obituary, a New York newspaper gave the account of his actions at the Battle of Bennington. His drum was destroyed by a bullet, and it tumbled down a hill. He immediately grabbed the rifle of a fallen comrade, charged the opposing line, captured an enemy drum, and returned to the battle. He later used that drum at the funeral of his friend General Ethan Allen.

The regiment performed well and was praised by General Gates. They were *the* key unit in cutting off General Burgoyne's retreat at Saratoga, which was a major early victory for the Continental Army. This victory probably convinced the king of France to support the colonies, and without this support we might not have won the war. This victory also motivated the Continental Congress to provide additional support to the army as they were close to abandoning the revolution due to several recent losses by General Washington. The regiment was recognized for their unusual tactics. These tactics are not unlike current Army Ranger tactics that use unconventional movements as opposed to frontal assaults. They could be very effective with few troops. I have read accounts that claimed Colonel Warner abandoned his troops during the Battle of Saratoga when it appeared they were losing the battle. That is a true claim, but the colonel returned to the battle with additional troops he had quickly raised in the neighborhood. They then won that battle. While this was a very large battle and many other American units were committed, it was an early turning point for the war.

The regiment was disbanded in December 1780, and David was discharged at that time. I cannot think of another single revolutionary regiment that contributed more to the American victory than the Green Mountain Boys. While this is a debatable assertion, it does make for interesting conversation, and I believe the facts support this stance. I believe the Perrigos were true fighting men. The Perrigo Papers alleged that prior to the war in Vermont, if they could not find a worthy opponent to fight, they would fight among themselves for entertainment.

We do not know where David is buried, but likely it is in Georgia Township in Franklin County, Vermont, which is near Highgate, Vermont, the location of his death. Accounts of his life show that, except for his military service, he never strayed further than twenty miles from the Lake Champlain area of western Vermont. He was born in New York, but that location is only a few miles from Pownal and across Lake Champlain.

Multiple sources were used to construct this story: the National Archives, the Perrigo Papers, interviews with Colonel Warner recorded by a reporter following the war, and the Missouri State Archives records. I believe the drum may be on exhibit in a Bennington County Historical Society museum.

Elijah Perrigo

Born: circa 1758

Died: 1840 in Rutland, Vermont

Birthplace: Skeensboro, Essex, New York

Married: Abigail Stewart 3 March 1791 in Clarendon, Rutland, Vermont

Buried: Unknown location in Vermont

Service: Warren's New York Regiment in the War of 1812

Elijah was the fifth-generation son of John Perrigo and his wife, Mary. He is listed in his father's will, which was read in 1812 in Essex, Chittenden, Vermont. I found no birth records for Elijah but will speculate that he was probably born in New York. His brothers David and Rufus claimed that location as their birthplace during their pension hearings. As discussed earlier, it is possible that their father moved to New York following his service in the French and Indian War. I am not certain about his birth date, but I believe he was born between the births of his brothers David and Rufus.

Elijah probably moved to Pownal with his father and later married Abigail Stewart on 3 March 1791 in Clarendon, Rutland County, Vermont. They were married by a justice of the peace, and the marriage was recorded on 20 March of that year. Abigail (1773–?) was the daughter of Oliver Cromwell Stewart Jr. and Jane Rhodes of Clarendon, Rutland, Vermont. This was a well-known early colonial family originally of Scotland. The spelling of this name varied from Stuart to Stewart to Steward. Steward was the original Scottish spelling of the name, and they were possibly descendants of Robert Bruce of Scotland.

Elijah signed a petition in 1794 requesting that the Vermont legislature repeal an act previously passed in 1787. This act required families to provide support to ministers, possibly including boarding them (*State Papers of Vermont, 1793–1796*, listed in the Reference Section).

Elijah and Abigail had seven children who were listed in his will:

- John, 1791–1850. Married Eliza Moffet, and they had five children. He spent most of his life in and around Burlington, Chittenden, Vermont.
- Clarissa M. Allen, 1797–1870. Married Steven Allen, and they had five children and lived in Saranac, Clinton, New York.
- Abigail Conger, 1800–1890. Married William Conger, and they had seven children and lived in Joliet, Illinois.
- Solomon, 1803–1880. Married Alzina Arnold, and they had eight children and lived in Beloit Rock, Wisconsin.

- Content Gardiner/Arnold, 1805–1880. She married Remington Gardiner and then Dyer Arnold Sr. and had two children by Dyer. She spent most of her life in Peru, Clinton, New York.
- Phillip, 1808–1880. He married Lucilla (last name unknown), and they had five children. He lived in Colden, Erie, New York.
- Branscom, 1812–1851. He married Betsy Burke, and they had six children. He lived in Schuyler Falls, Clinton, New York.

I found military records attesting to the fact that Elijah served in Warner's New York Regiment during the War of 1812. I was unable to prove the death date given above.

Corporal Rufus Perrigo

Born: 1761

Died: 7 June 1833 in St. Albans, Franklin, Vermont

Birthplace: Dover, New York

Married: (1) Prudence Annie Hurlburt and (2) Mary (last name unknown)

Buried: Unknown location in St. Albans, Franklin, Vermont

Service: Continental Line in the Green Mountain Boys and in the Vermont Militia

DAR: None

SAR: None

Rufus is a fifth-generation Perrigo and was the son of John Perrigo and Mary, whose last name is unknown. He is listed as a son in his father's 1812 will, but I found no birth records that might reveal his exact birth date or location. It is interesting to note that he made a pension request late in his life and gave a New York location as his birthplace. I placed his father in Pownal by 1765 and assumed he had lived in Massachusetts following the French and Indian War, with his children being born in Pownal. I was probably wrong. I now believe that his father remained in New York after his service in the French and Indian War, married there, and some of his children were born in Dover, New York, before the family moved to Pownal. Rufus signed at least one petition in Pownal and clearly lived there with his father and brother David prior to the Revolutionary War. I can place them there by 1765.

Rufus married Prudence Annie Hurlburt of Woodbury, Connecticut, in 1780. No marriage records were found. Prudence was probably a sister of Eunice, who married his brother David. I have seen genealogies that show Prudence died in 1790, but I have found no evidence of that. In 1832 he listed his wife as Mary at his pension hearing, so he possibly remarried after the death of Prudence.

His military service in the Revolutionary War is documented by the National Archives, and I have those records. During his 1831 pension request he stated there were four enlistments, and his official records seem to support that claim, except for the Warner Regiment. He summarized his enlistments in a written statement, and I will recount that statement.

He said he was born in Dover, New York, in 1761. He enlisted in Captain Fischer's company of the Vermont Militia in the month the British put a chain across the Hudson River (April 1778). He then helped construct the fort at West Point and then was discharged after serving his three-month enlistment as a private.

His next enlistment was under the command of Colonel Warner (this was the Green Mountain Boys), and then they marched to Ft. George and remained there for three months. During this period, the British and Indians came down to a place called Sabbath Island where they captured and scalped several soldiers. His term of enlistment was for three months, and he stated he served that time. Warner commanded the Green Mountain Boys, and his brother David was serving as a drummer in that storied regiment at the same time.

In the months of April and May 1780 he enlisted for ten months under the command of Captain William Hutcheon and Colonel Ebenezer Allen of the Vermont Militia and was stationed at Pittsforce and Castleton in Vermont. This would have been about thirty-five miles north of Pownal.

March 1781 saw him enlist in Captain Daniel Comstock's company and Colonel Fletcher's regiment of the Vermont Militia for nine months as a corporal. He was stationed at Ft. Newgrange at Pittsfield. He was a scout most of this enlistment and was discharged. His father also served in that regiment.

In all, he probably served at least twenty-four months in the revolution and was awarded a pension. That pension number is 19.028. He is also shown on the Vermont pensioners' roll starting in 1831 in Burlington.

His enlistment in the Warner Regiment is worth further discussion. This regiment was commanded by Colonel Seth Warner, and a detailed account of that regiment is recounted with his brother David's story above. What happened to Rufus in this unit is not certain but may have involved a dispute and a formal departure from the unit with buttons being cut off. That story may be lost to history, but Bob Bishop related some of that story in the Perrigo Papers. I should also mention I could not find the official military records supporting his enlistment in the storied Green Mountain Boys, but I do not doubt for one moment that he served in that unit. I also noted he did not swear that he had been honorably discharged from that unit as he did with his other Revolutionary War units during his pension hearings. I will also note that Bob Bishop was descended from this Perrigo line.

Rufus and his family did not stray far from Pownal during his life. He was living in Half-Moon, Albany County, New York, in 1790, which is just across the Vermont and New York state line (1790 census). From 1800 to 1810 he and his growing family lived in Willsboro, Essex, New York, and from 1810 to 1830 he was back in Vermont in Franklin where he lived until his death (military pension hearing statement). I found him in the Essex County, New York, tax rolls for 1804 being taxed for a house and farm. His brothers David and Silvester lived nearby. He was probably a farmer, and in 1832 he stated he was unable to work. His wife Mary outlived him and drew a pension. She would have been eligible for the pension even if she had not been married during the war because of the 1832 Pension Act.

I have found thirteen children of Rufus, but I do not know if their mother was Prudence or Mary:

- Alanson, 1789–1862. Married Abigail Coffey, and they had seven children. They lived in Highgate, Vermont, Lyme, and Clayton, New York.
- Lydia People, 1790–1868. Married Benjamin People and lived in Georgia Plains, Franklin, Vermont.
- David, 1793–Unknown death date.
- Eunice Muriel Beams, 1795–1876. Married Albert Irving Beams and lived in Franklin, New York.
- Joel, 1797–1866. Married Henrietta Sylvester, had six children, and settled in Milwaukee, Wisconsin.
- Sally Basford, 1797–1877. Married Benjamin Basford and lived in Saint Albans, Franklin, Vermont.
- Warren, 1801–1865. Married Delia Albin Allen. They had six children and settled in Milwaukee, Wisconsin.
- Meder, 1807–1906. Married (1) Lydia and (2) Ellen Gilbert and settled in Edgerton, Rock County, Wisconsin. He had ten children. Meder is the grandfather of Bob Bishop.
- Ada White, 1809–1891. Married John Kinney White and settled in Edgerton, Rock, Wisconsin.
- Prudence Shepard Gavin, 1811–1884. Married Ruben S. Shepard and lived in Georgia, Franklin, Vermont. She became a postmaster for Georgia.
- Delana Washburn, 1813–1886. Married John Washburn, had three children, and lived in Saint Albans, Franklin County, Vermont.
- William, 1814–1896. Married Hannah Eliza Little, had four children, and settled in Brooklyn, New York.
- Candice Conger, 1818–1888. Married Anson N. Conger, had three children, and lived in Saint Albans, Vermont.

I did not find a will or probate records for Rufus and was unable to find a burial location.

Dr. John Perrigo Jr.

Born: 1767
Died: 7 March 1820 in Burlington, Chittenden, Vermont
Birthplace: Unknown, but probably New York or Pownal, Vermont
Married: Almira Hitchcock in 1796 in Kingsbury, Washington, New York
Buried: Elmwood Cemetery, Burlington, Vermont
Service: Vermont Militia in company of Nathaniel Seeley's alarm men in the regiment commanded by Colonel Samuel Herrick beginning 11 October 1780
DAR: A089023
SAR: P-268709

Dr. John Perrigo Jr. is a fifth-generation Perrigo and the son of John Perrigo and his wife Mary (possibly Flint) of Pownal and then Clarendon, Rutland, Vermont. He is the brother of Rufus and David discussed above. The birthplace of Dr. John is not certain—it is most probably New York, but possibly Pownal, Vermont. His brothers David and Rufus gave New York as their birth state in their pension hearings, but his father had been a citizen of Pownal for several years prior to the war and signed a petition there in 1782 for the bridge discussed above. The DAR records his birthplace as New York but offers no evidence of that location except his marriage there. The 1790 census for his father shows him in Clarendon, Vermont. We know he is the son of John because of being listed in his father's will of 1811, and the fact that he signed a petition with his father in Pownal.

He married Almira Hitchcock in Kingsbury, Washington County, New York, in 1796, and they had six children. They were:

- Charles Herbert, 1796–1862. Became a lawyer and settled in Julien, Dubuque, Iowa.
- Mary Ann van Duzee, 1797–1867. Married and settled in Hastings, Minnesota.
- John Dean, 1801–1832. Married and remained in Burlington.
- Charlotte Smith White, 1804–1866. Married and settled in Viroqua, Vernon County, Wisconsin.
- Isaac Hitchcock, 1807–1875. Married and settled in Lockport, Niagara, New York.
- Minerva Martindale Goodrich, 1811–1862. Married and settled in Dubuque, Dubuque County, Iowa.

Dr. John served in the Revolutionary War for ten days, in the Vermont Militia. His unit was a unit of alarm men that was called to Burlington for a ten-day call up in October 1780.

He died on 7 March 1820 in Burlington at the age of fifty-three, and he is buried in the Elmwood Cemetery in Burlington. His probate case is interesting as his oldest son, Charles, was appointed administrator and was directed to quickly inventory the estate. Charles was about twenty-four years old, and the youngest child was about nine years old. After the inventory, it was discovered his estate was insolvent and the many bills could not be paid. The list of debts is many pages in length, with most amounts being under $10 and some several hundred. The probate judge directed that Charles make a list of what he recommended be paid to each person holding the debt. After one year, Charles discovered five acres of land owned by Dr. John, but that small parcel did not adequately cover the many debts. It is unclear how many dollars remained to support his wife and children after the estate was settled.

Medical practice in the early 1700s was no guarantee of financial success, as patients often did not or could not pay for services rendered. Country doctors often needed a source of income to support their medical practice. Land speculation was sometimes the solution.

Bob Bishop elaborated on these debts in the Perrigo Papers, and he was probably correct in that many individuals and families were indebted to Dr. John for various medical services he had delivered over his many years of practice. I noticed numerous debts owed to him in his son's accounting of his assets, but there were no descriptions of those amounts owed him. Those bills would never be collected.

Bishop also discussed the land speculation activities of Dr. John, and there seemed to be many. These activities would be interesting research for future projects, but I will not pursue those now.

The fact that two fifth-generation Perrigos have presented themselves as doctors in early New England poses some questions. Dr. Robert Perrigo Jr., son of Robert discussed above, was born in Rhode Island, moved to Argyle, New York, shortly after the revolution, and eventually moved to Pennsylvania. Dr. John Perrigo discussed here remained in the Rutland/Chittenden, Vermont, area for most of his remaining life. He did not stray far from Pownal. How did they obtain their medical training? We may never know the answer to this question, but it bears some research. Bob Bishop in the Perrigo Papers posed a similar question about Dr. John, who seemingly served as a doctor during the Revolutionary War. Bishop's response to his own question was there was a medical college located not far from Pownal in Vermont and that maybe he attended that college. Here is the result of some cursory research by me on that subject.

The book *The First Medical College in Vermont: 1818–1862*, shown in the Reference Section below, gives the history of this college in Castleton, Vermont. The college did not graduate its first doctors until around 1822 and was closed by 1862. The college had about 2,500 total students with maybe 1,400 completing the instruction. The list of graduates does not include anyone with the name of Perrigo, and I did not expect to find them on that list, given that Dr. John was dead in 1820 and Dr. Robert was in New York. Castleton is near the western border of Vermont, as is Pownal, which is several miles to the south near the Massachusetts border. The medical training received by Dr. John was soon after the revolution, and the Castleton college did not exist until forty years after that war. Dartmouth College in New York and the several colleges in Massachusetts were the choices. There were other choices for a young man of that era and location to obtain medical training and education, and I expect this was the route taken by both Dr. Robert and Dr. John Perrigo. The book referenced above explains that many doctors in the frontier regions were prepared for their careers through the "preceptor system." This was essentially an OJT process. There were no entrance requirements, except one can imagine that being able to read and write would be useful. Some prospective doctors already held a four-year degree in the arts. The referenced book explained that most students at this college in the early 1800s did not graduate before beginning their practice. Some attended only one term. Many did, however, possess a four-year general education degree before beginning training at the medical school. In the preceptor system, the student doctor paid the licensed doctor for training. The colonies did not issue licenses or issue standards for qualification to practice for several years.

Dr. John Perrigo, contrary to family legend, almost certainly did not serve as a doctor during his ten-day call up in 1780 in Burlington. He may well have been a practicing doctor at that time, but I found no records supporting that idea. In fact, the only evidence of his being a doctor is on his 1820 death certificate generated by the city of Burlington giving his name as Dr. John Perrigo Jr. In fairness, descendants of Dr. John seem to hold that he had a long medical career, and I have no reason to doubt that claim. More research is in order, as this is an interesting story. He was certainly a Patriot.

If Dr. Robert Perrigo received medical training at the college level, it was likely received in New York, due to his being less than twenty years old when he left Rhode Island. There were several medical colleges in New York at that time, and maybe he attended there, or perhaps he studied under another doctor. Again, he was a Patriot, and we owe both him and Dr. John Perrigo much.

I think these were intelligent and brave men, and I believe their lives and contributions deserve more research to document their contributions. They just did what they could.

Silvester Perrigo

Born: 1768

Died: 7 March 1820 in Burlington, Chittenden, Vermont

Birthplace: Pownal, Bennington, Vermont

Married: (1) Hannah Dawley (1778–1804) on 10 July 1794 and (2) Amarilla (last name unknown) on 17 March 1803

Buried: Unknown location probably in Burlington, Vermont

Service: None known

DAR: None

SAR: None

Silvester is a fifth-generation Perrigo and son of John Perrigo and Mary of Pownal, Vermont. This is a proven relationship as he is listed in his father's will of 1812. The New York 1804 Tax List shows him living in proximity to his brothers Rufus and David and his cousin Frederick. His taxes were for a shop owned by him, and the others for a house and farm.

This Silvester married Hannah Dawley on 10 July 1794 in Mount Holly, Vermont. We believe he later married Amarilla (last name unknown) on 17 March 1803 in Monkton, Addison, Vermont. I was unable to document any children from either of these marriages. His death date is not proven.

Frederick Howard Perrigo

Born: 10 April 1765

Died: 26 December 1850 in Ellenburg, Clinton, New York

Birthplace: Pownal, Bennington, Vermont

Married: Mary "Polly" Van Ornam on 16 April 1791 in Charlotte, Chittenden, Vermont

Buried: Unknown location

Service: Revolutionary War from 1 July 1781 to 26 November 1781 in Fletcher's Regiment of the Vermont Militia as a private. He also served in the New York Twenty-Ninth Infantry during the War of 1812.

DAR: A 089012

SAR: None

Frederick is a fifth-generation Perrigo and the son of David Perrigo and Susanna Varrel of Pownal, Bennington, Vermont. This is an unproven relationship as with his brother Justus Sr., discussed next. As has been previously discussed, their Pownal connection is strong for several reasons, and they certainly do not fit in the John Perrigo family group of Pownal. As discussed with his father's story above, I believe that his father lived with him when the 1800 Vermont census was taken, with Justus, Sr. living nearby. Statements by him during his pension hearings and by his family seem to prove he was born in Pownal.

Frederick married Mary "Polly" Van Ornam on 16 April 1791 in Chittenden, Vermont. This marriage took place after he had served in the Revolutionary War in the Vermont Militia under the command of Colonel Fletcher. I did not find their marriage records; however, they both testified for one of his pension hearings that they had been married by a justice of the peace in Charlotte, Vermont, in 1791. I noticed from the pension hearings that Frederick could read and write, but Mary could not.

He served in the same Revolutionary War unit as his cousin Rufus. He served about ten months and was discharged in November 1781. The dates of service shown above are recovered from his records, which I have. The claim of ten months comes from many sworn statements from Frederick and fellow soldiers during his pension hearings.

He joined the New York Twenty-Ninth Infantry Regiment in 1813 and served about six months. During this service he was severely injured by a fall from a horse while spreading an alert notice at night. He was discharged about four months later because of his inability to perform his duties. This injury severely affected his ability to work for the remainder of his life and was the justification for the applications for his pension by his wife after his death.

His National Archives files for pension claims are extensive, with more than two hundred pages that I discovered. The New York Militia apparently never declared that Frederick had been disabled, as with his brother Justus Sr., who had been injured in combat.

It appears that he filed for disability in early 1830, but after several requests for additional information, the application was rejected. He obtained a doctor's certification that he was truly disabled, and several witness statements were included attesting to the fact that he had been injured while performing his duties.

After his death, his wife applied for a pension and for a land bounty. She quickly was awarded a $30/year pension for the remainder of her life as well as a 160-acre land grant. It appears that she obtained the services of a lawyer in this instance as she left written instructions for the land grant to be forwarded to her attorney when it was granted. I could find no record of where this grant was to be awarded. The pension number was W 26858.

During the several hearings pertaining to his Revolutionary War claims, he provided some interesting information about where he spent his life until 1823. He said he was born in Pownal on 10 April 1765 and that after the Revolutionary War he remained in Pownal until 1785, when he moved to a town in Massachusetts until 1788. He then moved to Willsboro, New York, until 1805 and then moved to Peru, New York, until 1810. He then moved back to Willsboro until 1813, when he enlisted, and then back to Peru until 1823. It appears that he later moved to Ellensburg in Clinton County, New York, and remained there until his death. The claim of being in Willsboro from 1788 until 1805 is consistent with the tax records of 1802 and 1803 and the 1800 federal census. I believe his father, David, lived with him until his death in 1803.

Frederick may have kept written records, as during the pension hearings he relayed the names of all eleven of their children, the dates and times of their birth, and the weather conditions. This was useful in researching their family histories due to the lack of birth records in Vermont. His children were:

- Dorcus Brownson/Ames, 1791–1879. She married Brownson (first name unknown) and later Edward Ames. She had five children and remained in Willsboro the rest of her life.
- Nancy, 1793–Unknown death date.
- Clara "Clarey," 1795–Unknown death date.
- Mary, 1797–1803. Died as a youth.
- Sarah A. (Sally) Moore, 1800–1864. Married Elias Moore and lived in Clinton, New York.
- William Alexander, 1802–1873. Married Mary Ann Shepard. They had eight children and remained in Clinton County, New York. He was a day laborer, but his son William became a doctor.
- James Drake, 1803–1833. Married Sarah Ann French, and they had ten children and remained in Clinton County, New York. He was a farm laborer.
- Robert Adair Bell, 1806–1861. Moved to Montreal, Canada, in 1825 and married Laura Julia Dunning, and they had five children. He remained in Canada.
- Charles Jefferson, 1808–1904. Married Mina Manzer—one son, Ernest, found. He remained in Clinton County.
- Frederick Howard Jr., 1810–1884. Married Charlotte Temple Ash. They had ten children and settled in Montcalm, Michigan.
- Marian, 1813–1813. Died as an infant.

I could find no will or probate records for Frederick, and his burial location in unknown. I think it was quite unfortunate that his injuries consisted mainly of a rupture in his stomach area—these injuries are today very treatable, sometimes on an outpatient basis.

Sergeant Justus J. Perrigo Sr.
Born: 23 April 1768
Died: 9 April 1832 on the Mississippi River south of Memphis
Birthplace: Pownal, Bennington County, New York
Married: First marriage not found; (2) Mary Andrews in August 1823 in Illinois
Buried: Unknown location
Service: War of 1812 in the Twenty-Third U.S. Infantry Regiment

Justus was born on 23 April 1768 in Pownal, Bennington, Vermont, to David Perrigo and Susanna Varrel and is a fifth-generation Perrigo. As discussed previously, this is an unproven relationship, but the evidence is strong that he is the son of David of Pownal. His statements made at the time of enlistment and pension filing establish this birth date and his being born in Pownal, Vermont.

His middle name is unknown. He used "J." at the time of his military enlistment and for his pension claim and several other official transactions. Perhaps his middle name was James, but that is a guess. I added the Sr. suffix to reduce possible confusion with his son Justus. As a matter of information, I have found no evidence that his son Justus ever used the middle initial of "J."

He was married prior to the birth of his first son Dudley, but we do not have the name of his first wife or any other information about her. Their marriage was likely by a justice of the peace, as with some of his siblings, and those records have not survived. All his children were born in New York prior to his move to Illinois. We do not know if his wife was alive when he departed, and if not, who might have cared for his young children.

He enlisted in the Twenty-Third U.S. Infantry Regiment at Manlius, New York, for the duration of the war. His company commander was Captain Fredrick Brawns, and the regimental commander was Colonel James Preston. He was wounded in combat three times. First was on 27 May 1813 at Ft. George, Upper Canada, with a gunshot wound to his left leg. The second injury was on 25 July 1814 at Bridgewater, New York, with a bayonet would. The third injury was from a bomb on 17 September 1814 at Ft. Eric. He received an honorable discharge because of those wounds and was declared fully disabled.

He soon received a large pension settlement of $2,617.17 (pension number 15202) on 16 April 1816 and a 160-acre land grant (warrant number 15.202). Portions of Adams County, Illinois (it may have been Pike County at the time), were set aside for war grants, and Justus wasted little time in making the move. I believe he was in Adams County by 1817 or 1818. Early newspaper articles sometimes focused on Justus as he was recognized as the first settler in Adams County. His farm was in Fall Creek Township, which is only a few miles south and east of present-day Quincy. His land was not far from the Mississippi River, but not the easily flooded bottomland. Great farmland today.

His trip from New York was not a minor undertaking immediately following the War of 1812, especially for a man with disabilities. I have studied the route of other family members leaving Pennsylvania en route to Missouri in the 1830s, and the first National Road from the Reading, Pennsylvania, area to Vandalia, Illinois, was established by 1837. This would have been a likely land route after 1830. This was a collection of several trails established by Indian tribes and explorers that linked major towns and cities along the way. Pre-1820 would have been an entirely different matter. Another option would have included traveling via the Ohio and Mississippi River, a more likely choice. Much of the Ohio River consisted of gauntlets of unhappy Native Americans. I have written of a particular family group (Gist) of my ancestors being captured while on this route in about 1818.

Justus was nearly fifty years old at the time of this journey, so he was a tough guy. We may never know the route taken by him, but the $2,600 military pension settlement would have bought a ticket by ship to New Orleans and then paid fare up the Mississippi. To be clear, there were other overland routes available in the early 1800s, the Natchez Trace route being one of them. (Meriwether Lewis died on the Natchez Trace trail.) Still a tough ride for an aging man with injuries and disabilities.

A newspaper article told the story he related to his prospective second wife. He bragged about having two thousand apple trees with many apples. She apparently bought in on that idea and was soon in Adams County and married to Justus. He was partly honest about the apple trees, but they were crabapple trees. The Perrigo Papers also related this story. This story is from *The History of Adams County* listed in the Reference Section.

Justus Sr. had eight children; Mary Andrews was not their mother:

- Dudley Scott, 1793–1880. Born in Fulton County, New York, married Lydia A. Hughes, and they had three children. He was in Adams County, Illinois, by 1825 and farmed in Adams County then Pike County. He had a second marriage to Cynthia Allen.
- Nellie, 1795–Unknown death date. She was born in Fulton County, New York.
- Nancy Jane, 1797–1881. Little is known of her.
- David, 1797–1875. Born in Fulton County, New York. He married Angelina Summerset in Indiana and later farmed in Urbana, Monroe, Iowa.
- Johnathan (John), 1812–1880. Born in Fulton County, New York, and married Mary Keokuk in Indiana and was in Adams County, Illinois, by 1840. He later settled and farmed in Clark County, Missouri. He had other marriages.
- William, 1813–1880. Born in New York and settled in Clark County, Missouri.
- Riley, 1814–1880. Born in Fulton County, New York, and settled in Clark County, Missouri.
- Justus Jr., 1816–1888. Born in Fulton County, New York, and married Rebecca Ann Payton in Adams County, Illinois, in 1832. They had eight children and remained in Adams County. Civil War soldier and my third great-grandfather.

I believe all his children were born in or around Fulton County, New York, with Justus Jr. being the last to be born in 1816, probably about the time of his departure for Illinois. The name of their mother and her death date may be lost to history. I do not know who cared for these children until they moved west. I believe Justus Sr. was dead by the time any of them made that journey, with exception of his oldest son, Dudley.

I have previously used 23 October 1832 as the death date for Justus, but I revised that date after investigation of his death. The October date was based on the date of his probate case filed by his son Dudley in Adams County, Illinois. It was reported he died in a steamboat accident on the Mississippi

River. My research has found only one such accident on the Mississippi River that year. In fact, there were few major accidents on the Mississippi River for another six or eight years. The river traffic was apparently light until 1838–1840, after which there were hundreds of such disasters on the Mississippi and Ohio Rivers. This accident occurred on 9 April 1832 as the boat passed through Arkansas about fifty miles south of Memphis. I had always assumed Justus had traveled to St. Louis on a business trip, but his journey must have been to New Orleans, with the accident occurring on the return trip at night. He would have likely changed ships at Memphis to continue to Quincy, as this boat was bound for Louisville, but that part of the trip was cut short. Here is the story I discovered:

He was likely aboard the *Brandywine*, a 432-ton steamboat that left New Orleans, Louisiana, on 3 April 1832 with a full load of cargo and 145 passengers and crew members bound for Louisville, Kentucky. On the evening of 9 April, the pilot, Benjamin T. Head, discovered several carriage wheels and parts packed in straw for transport had caught fire on the vessel's hurricane deck. The captain and crew tried to toss the burning cargo overboard, and a crew member attempted to douse the flames with water, but they were forced back by the fierce flames. There were high winds, and it was impossible to contain the fire, so the captain tried to run the *Brandywine* ashore, but it became stuck on a sandbar in nine feet of water. He said there were three minutes from the time the fire was discovered to when it was impossible to remain on the boat. Passengers crowded to one side of the boat to escape, and the boat capsized, throwing them into the water. The boilers then exploded after being starved of water from the leaning of the boat. Many passengers were killed instantly from the explosion and many from drowning in the river at night.

An 1856 account of the disaster alleged that the vessel was racing another steamboat, the *Hudson*, at the time of the accident. This account claimed that, for the purpose of producing more intense heat and thus accelerating the boat's speed, a large quantity of rosin had been thrown into the furnaces, and the flames then left the smokestacks and ignited the straw and wood wheels located on the deck.

Possibly 76 of the 145 people on board survived the disaster. This story was taken from the CALS Encyclopedia of Arkansas website.

Lloyd's Steamboat Directory, shown in the Reference Section, also has an account of the wreck that matches the CALS description discussed above. This report lists the names of those killed from the explosion and fire, but Justus is not among that list. The report also states that the account does not contain the names of those taken to shore for care of their injuries that later died or those lost in the water with bodies never recovered. The list contains only twenty-six of about seventy-five of those losing their lives.

Following his death, his second wife, Mary, filed to receive military benefits based on his service. She claimed he had fought in the Revolutionary War and had been injured. That request was denied for the reason that he had already received a settlement.

Charles Perrigo

Born: 1770

Died: 1856 in Addison, Steuben, New York

Birthplace: Pownal, Bennington, Vermont

Married: Laura Ward (1787–1870) in New York

Buried: Unknown location probably in Steuben, New York

Service: None known

DAR: None

SAR: None

Charles is the son of David Perrigo and Susanna Varrel of Pownal, Vermont, and is a fifth-generation family member. This is an unproven relationship. In 1791, he married Laura Ward (1787–1870), the daughter of Ruben Ward and Jemima Tiffany in Vermont. Ruben was a Revolutionary War Patriot and Jemima was an ancestor of the well-known Tiffany family of New York. The relationship of Laura to the Tiffany family is documented in the book *The Tiffanys of America* (page 161), shown in the Reference Section. Laura's marriage to Charles is also documented on the same page.

Laura's mother, Jemima (1761–1848), was the daughter of Samuel Tiffany, originally of Old Lyme, Connecticut, the original hometown of the Robert Perrigo family. Her father, Ruben (1748–1825), fought in the Revolutionary War as a corporal in Captain Van Ness's company of the First New York Regiment. The Wards lived in Delaware County, New York, as did Charles and Laura.

Charles graduated from the University of Vermont School of Agriculture in 1815 in Burlington, Vermont. He is listed on page 252 with the graduates of that university in the college catalog included in the Reference Section below.

He lived in Hamden, Delaware County, New York, for much of his remaining life. The federal census reports of 1820,1830, and 1840 show him in Delaware County. The 1830 census reports six children of the household under the age of twenty, as their seventh child, Orson, was not yet born. He and Laura had seven children:

- Laura Susan Stevens, 1813–1880. Married James Stevens and settled in Dalton, Muskegon, Michigan.
- Amanda Orinda Wood, 1817–Unknown death date. She married Asa Wood.
- Lyman, 1820-1870.
- Jemima Julia Bailey, 1824–1898. She married Luther Bailey and lived in Mount Pleasant, New York.
- Dorcus Ashley, 1829–1904. She married Lewis Ashley, and they lived in Halfmoon, Saratoga, New York. This is near Pownal, Vermont.

- William H., 1830–1900. He married Susan A. Sands, and they lived in Osceola, Tioga, Pennsylvania.
- Orson W., 1836–1920. He married Mary Jane Edwards, and they lived in Genoa, Cayuga, New York.

Daughter Laura's death certificate listed her mother as Laura.

After the death of Charles in 1856, Laura married Robert Finch, also of Steuben, New York, in 1860. His first wife had recently died in 1859. Laura then moved with Robert to Osceola, Tioga County, Pennsylvania, where she lived until her death in 1870.

Chapter Seven

The intent of this project has been to take a close look at the first five generations of the American Perrigo family and identify Justus Perrigo Sr's father. Associated with that mission was my intent to discover and tell some of the stories of this very interesting family through the lens of historical events. Along the way, I identified more than fifty family groups in the five generations as well as two added English generations. I also included the names and dates of the sixth generation to aid in future family research.

I remain indebted to Professor Robert Bishop for the work he and other contributors to the Perrigo Papers made more than forty years ago. While I did not always agree with Bob on some of the relationships presented in those papers, that should surprise no one, as family research has changed. Technology improvements have aided family research in many ways beyond the obvious availability of several genealogy research platforms. Consider the fact that Bob used a typewriter and steno paper. I enjoyed the availability of several large family genealogy libraries that I believe did not exist in 1980. I was able to build a rather large personal library of online reference books that greatly aided in research for this project. Most of those documents and books existed then, but in limited numbers, and they were in many locations Bob would not have readily accessed.

New England was a history-rich environment during this era, and the Perrigo family was close to many of those events we all studied in school. From the *Mayflower* in 1620 to King Philip's War, the French and Indian War, and the revolution, the Perrigos and extended family were more than involved, they were committed. Thirteen Revolutionary War Patriots says it all.

There were some pleasant surprises. I did not expect the discovery of an unknown-to-me Missouri Perrigo line. This line, beginning with the New Jersey Ezekiel Perrigo line, migrated across New Jersey, Pennsylvania, Ohio, and on to Iowa and Missouri. Neither the Perrigo Papers nor the Cutter Account explored this family line. I certainly did not expect the discovery of *Mayflower* ancestors. There were two, and they were well-known early citizens of Plymouth Colony. Figures 11 and 12 below reflect historic homes left by those first Americans. I will mention that the original Plymouth Bradford home was next door to the Alden home, but as that home no longer stands, I chose to display the Bradford Rhode Island plantation home. Further information appears on page 70.

There is unfinished business. One of the original purposes of this project was that of finding the father of Justus Perrigo Sr. While I am confident that I have it right, proof remains elusive. I believe that the lack of vital records keeping by both the city and churches of Pownal prior to the Revolutionary War contributed to this shortfall. I believe that those birth records do not exist; not only for Justus Sr. but for other fifth-generation Pownal citizens. I am hopeful that David's will or probate records, when found, will perhaps offer a solution to the question.

The James and David Perrigo relationship remains unproven. There is strong evidence of the correctness of this assertion; however, I am not hopeful of an easy solution in this relationship problem. Despite the excellent record-keeping in early Massachusetts, this birth seems to have never been recorded. I have offered a likely explanation to this problem, but further research will be necessary. I have focused on birth records, and they are simple—those Massachusetts towns were small, and they recorded few births in any given year. They are readily available from at least three sources: original, microfiche copies, and published compilations from the originals. I have used all available sources with no matches. Future research must focus on tax and other local records.

I believe the collation of James, David, and John in early Pownal—as well as James and David's military service during the revolution in the same unit—establishes a strong family relationship. Remember, the James and John relationship is proven. Remember also that David and John served in the same unit during the French and Indian War and enlisted together. This fact seems to further strengthen the family relationship claim.

In spite of lack of some important documentation, the Perrigo family is indeed an interesting family of historical significance, and I am honored to be a descendant of that family line that has contributed so much to our history. I hope that these stories will help other family descendants research their relationship to this family.

FIGURE 11: The John Alden Home of Duxbury, Plymouth, Massachusetts

Source: Wikimedia Commons, 15 March, Pete Forsyth

FIGURE 12: The Governor William Bradford House in Bristol, Rhode Island
(Refer to page 70 for additional information.)

Source: Wikimedia Commons, 31 August 2013, Kenneth C. Zirkel

Reference Section

Books, Published and unpublished articles, Records of note:

This list contains published, unpublished, and official records:

The Brett Genealogy, Parts I, II and III. Compiled by L.B. Goodenow. Murray Emory and Company, Cambridge, Massachusetts, 1915.

Court Summons to Henry Peterson regarding the probate of the will of Robert Perrigo – 1719. London county court records held in the Connecticut State Library in Hartford. Used to establish the children of Robert and their locations as well as several grandchildren.

Cutter Account: *Genealogical and Family History of Northern New York*, Volume I. William Richard Cutter. Page 1169. Note: I refer to this as the Cutter Account in the book.

Descendants of Governor William Bradford: Through the First Seven Generations. Hill, Ruth Gardner. United States, Unknown, 1951. Documents Alice Webb Perrigo (wife of Ezekiel) as a *Mayflower* Descendant. Refer to the documents listed below for the *Mayflower* passenger list.

Documents Relating to the Colonial History of the State of New Jersey, Volume XXII: Marriage Records 1665–1800. Edited by William Nelson. Peterson, New Jersey. The Press Printing Company, 269 Main St., 1900.

"Doty Tavern." Daniel T.V. Huntoon, *Potter's American Monthly*, July 1876, vol. 7 no. 5, pages 24–26. Used for the James Perrigo story.

The First Medical College in Vermont: 1818–1862. Frederick Clayton Waite, Vermont Historical Society, 1919. Vermont Printing Company, Brattleboro, Vermont.

A Gazetteer of Vermont: Containing Descriptions of all the Counties, Towns, and Districts in the State. John Hayward. Boston: Tappan, Whittenmore, and Mason, 114 Washington Street, 1849.

Genealogical and Family History of Northern New York, Volume I. William Richard Cutter. Page 1169. Note: I refer to this as the Cutter Account in the book.

Genealogical Guide to the Early Settlers of America: With a Brief History of Those of the First Generation. Henry Whittmore, Clearfield Company, 1994. Reprinted from *The Spirit of 76*. This provided information on the marriages of both Ezekiel and Robert Perrigo Jr. as well as their service in Queen Anne's War.

"Historic Hastings." J. Manning F.S.A. Parish Clerk of All Saints and St. Clements and onetime curator of the Hastings Museums, 1986. Published by Cinque Port Press, Ltd. St. Leonards-on-the-Sea, East Sussex, England. This document provided information on both John Perigoe and his father Robert Perigoe and their occupations.

The History of Adams County, Illinois. R.W. Miles. Murray, Williams, and Phelps. Chicago, Illinois. Chapter IX, page 397. Used for the Justus J. Perrigo Sr. story.

History of the Colony of New Haven, before and after the Union with Connecticut. Edward R. Lambert, New Haven. Printed and published by Hitchcock and Stafford, 1838.

History of the First Baptist Church of Wantage, Sussex, New Jersey. Revised by Rev. George F. Love in 1874 and by James Bristow in 1903. Copy made by Mrs. Jannie Little Meaker in 1931. This is in possession of the New Jersey Historical Society, 230 Broadway, Newark, New Jersey. Note: This was the Perrigo family church from 1750 until the mid-1800s. The list contains the names and various religious events involving that family.

History of Middlesex County, Connecticut, with biographical sketches. J.B. Beers and Company, 36 Vesey St., New York, 1884.

History of Windham County, Connecticut. Richard M. Bayles. New York, W.W. Preston, 1889. Contains facts of contributions and family information on Sergeant John Royce and Sarah Perrigo, daughter of Robert Sr.

Lloyd's Steamboat Directory. The Clerk's Office of the District Court for the Eastern District of Pennsylvania. Printed by Jesper Harding, Philadelphia. Entered according to Act of Congress. Used to establish Justus J. Perrigo's death date.

Luke Gridley's Diary of 1757. Luke Gridley. The Acorn Society. This published diary recounts some events of the Connecticut unit at Fort Ticonderoga and the accidental death of John Kemp Perrigo.
Massachusetts Officers and Soldiers in the French and Indian Wars 1755–1756. Edited by David Goss and David Zarowin.

Massachusetts Officers and Soldiers, 1702–1722: Queen Anne's War to Dummer's War. Edited by Mary E. Donahue. The Society of Colonial Wars in the Commonwealth of Massachusetts. The Office of the Secretary of the Commonwealth of Massachusetts, Archives Division. The New England Historic Genealogy Society.

Massachusetts Soldiers and Sailors of the Revolutionary War, Volumes 1–17. Boston, Massachusetts, Secretary of the Commonwealth, Massachusetts. Wright and Potter Printing, 1896–1908.

Mayflower Births and Deaths: From the Files of George Ernest Bowman at the Society of Mayflower Descendants, Volumes I and II. Susan L. Rosen. Genealogical Publishing Company, Inc., 1992.

Mayflower Compact: "Signers of the Mayflower Compact." Published by the *Mail and Express* newspaper of New York, 12, 19, and 26 November and 24 December 1898.

Mayflower passenger list: Documents for the *Mayflower* passenger list for the Honorable John Alden, second great-grandfather of Lydia Hayward, wife of James Perrigo Sr.

Memorial of the Descendants of the Honorable John Alden. Ebenezer Alden. Randolph, Massachusetts, 1687, pages 1 and 2.

Minutes of the Court of Burgomasters and Schepens, Volume 4, 1663. These proceedings document a lawsuit brought against Sarah Perrigo, wife of Robert, who had attached tobacco to obtain payment of a debt owed her.

New England Historical & Genealogical Register 1847–2011. Online database. Provo, Utah, USA: Ancestry.com Operations, Inc. 2011. Compiled from *The New England Historical and Genealogical Register*, Boston, The New England Historic and Genealogical Society. Lists first-generation Robert Perrigo's daughters and their mothers.

North American Family Histories 1500–2000. Provo, Utah, 2016, page 564.

"The Perrigo Papers." Compiled by Professor Robert E. Bishop of Bradenton, Florida. Volume I and II from 1980 to 1982. Digitized copy of all the issues is in my possession. This is an unpublished, public domain record.

The Record of Births, Marriages and Deaths and Intentions of Marriage in the Town of Stoughton and the Town of Canton from 1727 to 1845. Canton, Massachusetts. Printed by William Bense, 1896. This book contains the town vital records of the James Perrigo family, including James and Lydia's marriage, sons Robert and James Jr.'s births, as well as son James Jr.'s marriage intention to Elizabeth Dickerman.

Regimental Book: Rhode Island Regiment for 1781 &c. Bruce C. MacGunnigle. Rhode Island Society of the Sons of the American Revolution, 2011.

Revolutionary War pension applications of David, Rufus, and Frederick H. Perrigo. National Archives.

Rolls of Connecticut Men in the French and Indian War, 1755–1762, Volumes I and II. Collections of the Connecticut Historical Society, Volume IX. Hartford, published by the society in 1903.

Saybrook at the Mouth of the Connecticut River: The First One Hundred Years. Gilman C. Gates. Copyright 1935 by Gilman C. Gates. Describes the geographic setting and events during Robert Perrigo's life there.

Soldiers, Sailors, and Patriots of the Revolutionary War, Vermont. Major General Carleton Edward Fisher and Sue Fisher. Picton Press, Camden, Maine.

The State of Vermont Rolls of the Soldiers of the Revolutionary War 1775–1783. Published by the Authority of the Legislature and compiled by the Vermont Historical Society.

State Papers of Vermont, Vol. 8, General Petitions 1778–1787. Edward Hoyt, Editor, Edward E. Armstrong, Secretary of State, Montpelier, Vermont, 1952. Pages 67–77. Signatures of James Perrigo Sr. and his sons David and John are included.

State Papers of Vermont, Vol. 10: General Petitions, 1793–1796. Edited by Allen Soule. Howard E. Armstrong, Secretary of State, Montpelier, Vermont, 1958. This book shows that Elijah Perrigo signed a petition requesting that the state repeal legislation that seemed to restrict religious freedoms.

The Tiffanys of America. Nelson Otis Tiffany. Buffalo: Mathews-Northrup, 1901. Documents the relationship of Laura Ward Perrigo to the well-known American Tiffany family.

"The Trials and Tribulations of Robert Perrigoe." *Sussex Family Historian*, vol. 11, #1. J.A. Beaden, Abbotts Mead, Earl Down, East Sussex. Published March 1994. This article recounts the life and legal problems of Robert Perrigoe of Sussex, England.

**University of Vermont State Agricultural College, Bennington, Vermont 1791–1890.* Burlington Free Press 1890. Used in the Charles Perrigo story.

Vermont 1771 Census. Jay Mack Holbrook. Holbrook Research Institute, Oxford Massachusetts, 1982. This census records the residence of Pownal for the year of 1765, which included James Sr., John, and David Perrigo.

The Vital Records of Wrentham, Massachusetts, to the Year 1850, Volume I: Births. Compiled by Thomas W. Baldwin AB. BS. Member of the New England Historic Genealogy Society. Boston, Mass. 1920. This is a compilation of vital records of Wrentham and contains records of the James Perrigo Jr. family as well as his children and their families.

Warning Out in New England 1656–1817. Josiah Henry Benton, LL.D. Boston: W.B. Clarke Company, 1911. This book discusses the New England practice of "warning out" and was used in the research of the James and Robert Perrigo stories.

Images:

FIGURE 1: Massachusetts Bay Colony 1630–1691. Wikimedia Commons. Kmusser 27 September 2005. Used under the Creative Commons Attribution-Share Alike 3.0 license. No changes were made to this image. **Permission:** *This file is licensed under the Creative Commons Attribution-Share Alike 3.0 Unported License.*

FIGURE 2: New England Map. Alamy H2DGRG.jpg. Used under licensing agreement with Alamy on 24 January 2023. No changes were made to this map.

FIGURES 3: Five Generations of the Perrigo Family Tree. Produced by the author.

FIGURES 4 and 5: "Historic Hastings," J. Manning F.S.A. Parish Clerk of All Saints and St. Clements and one-time curator of the Hastings Museums, 1986. Published by Cinque Port Press, Ltd. St. Leonards-on-the-Sea, East Sussex, England.

FIGURE 6: Old Lyme, New London County, Connecticut Map. 27 July 2012. Public Domain Map based on original of Michael J. Leclerc. Provided by Wikimedia. No changes were made to this map.

FIGURE 7: Massachusetts U.S. Town and Vital Records, Bridgewater, Plymouth, Massachusetts, 1620–1988. The James Perrigo "warning out." Reproduced by the author from the original Bridgewater City record of the event.

FIGURE 8: Massachusetts County Map. Provided by Wikimedia Commons. 25 April 2010. Used under the Creative Commons Attribution-Share Alike 3.0 license. No changes were made to this image. **Permission:** *This file is licensed under the Creative Commons Attribution-Share Alike 3.0 Unported License.*

FIGURE 9: James Perrigo Jr. Clock.

FIGURE 10: James Perrigo III Clock. Image obtained from Skinner Auctions, Inc. www. skinnerauctions.com.

FIGURE 11: John Alden home of Plymouth, Massachusetts. Provided by Wikimedia Commons. 15 March 2009. Pete Forsyth. Used under the Creative Commons Attribution-Share Alike 3.0 license. No changes were made to this image.

FIGURE 12: Mount Hope Farm, the home of Governor William Bradford, Bristol, Rhode Island. Provided by Wikimedia Commons. 31 August 2013. Kenneth C. Zirkel. Used under the Creative Commons Attribution-Share Alike 3.0 license. No changes were made to this image.

Index to Military References

Index to Names

*(Birth years are included with certain confusing entries.
Maiden names are enclosed in brackets for clarity.
Names in parentheses are alternate names or spellings.)*

Miller,

    Anna [Stratton] Miller, 68

    Joseph M., 68

    Mary Jane [Miller] Perego, 64

Minich,

    Helen [Minich] Perego, 65

Moffet

    Eliza [Moffet] Perrigo, 82

Moore,

    Elias, 90

    Sarah A. (Sally) [Perrigo] Moore, 90

Mullins,

    Priscilla Sarah [Mullins] Alden, 30

Myers,

    John William, 68

    Margaret [Stratton], 68

Nancy,

    Anna [Nancy] Perrigo, 75

Nichols

    Isabel [Nichols] Perrigo, 71

Page,

    Hannah [Page] Perrigo, 78

Parlett,

    Elizabeth Ann [Parlett] Perrigo, 79

Parmenter,

    Alfred, 68

    Sarah [Stratton], 68

Payton,

    Rebecca Ann, 92

Peck,

    Joseph, 20

People,

    Lydia [Perrigo], 85

    People, Benjamin, 85

Perego, *see also* **Perrigo, Perigoe,**

Perego,

    Amanda [Perego] Harrington, 65

    Florence, 65

    Helen [Minich], 65

    Isaac, *b.1856,* 65

    Isaac, *b. 1801,* 64

    James, *b.1849,* 65

    James, *b.1776,* 64

    John, *b.1815,* 64

    Joseph, *b.1864,* 65

    Margret [Perego] Grier, 64

    Maria Jane [Perego] Lanning, 65

    Martha Jane [Williams], 65

    Matilda Samantha [Clary], 64

    Nancy [Perego] Ward, 64

    Permila [Perego] Wilson Bourner, 65

    Samuel Greenbury, *b.1855,* 65

    Sarah [Perego] Galloway, 64

    Sarah/Sadie [Perego] DePriest, 65

    William Henry, *b.1852,* 65

Perigoe, *see also* **Perrigo, Perego,**

Perigoe,

    Amie Gregorye Scott, 11

    John, b.1588, 11, 102

    Robert, b. cir.1560, 11, 102

    Martha Gabryell, 11

Perrigo, *see also* **Perego, Perigoe,**

Perrigo,

    Abel *b.1773,* 43, 61, 62, 63, 64, 66, 67, 69, 72,

    Abigail [Brock], 47, 55, 58, 70, 72

    Abigail [Coffey], 85

    Abigail [Perrigo] Conger, 82

    Abigail [Perrigo] Fouseur, 26

    Abigail [Stewart], 82

    Abigail, *b.1791,* 71

    Abigail, *b.1681,* 12, 24

    Abigail, *b.1767,* 47

    Ada [Perrigo] White, 85

    Adelide [Perrigo] Townsend, 63

    Alanson, 85

    Allice [Elsey], 18, 19, 25, 26, 27

    Alice or Alis Elsie, 18, 19

    Alice [Webb], 70, 71, 101

    Allice Else, 26

    Almira [Hitchcock], 85, 86,

    Alzina [Arnold], 82

    Amanda [Perego] Harrington, 65

    Amanda Orinda [Perrigo] Wood, 94

    Amarilla [maiden name unknown], 88

www.ingramcontent.com/pod-product-compliance
Lightning Source LLC
Chambersburg PA
CBHW050619110426
42813CB00010B/2616